Centre for Educational Research and Innovation (CERI)

Schools and Business:
a new partnership

ORGANISATION FOR ECONOMIC CO-OPERATION AND DEVELOPMENT

ORGANISATION FOR ECONOMIC CO-OPERATION AND DEVELOPMENT

Pursuant to Article 1 of the Convention signed in Paris on 14th December 1960, and which came into force on 30th September 1961, the Organisation for Economic Co-operation and Development (OECD) shall promote policies designed:

— to achieve the highest sustainable economic growth and employment and a rising standard of living in Member countries, while maintaining financial stability, and thus to contribute to the development of the world economy;
— to contribute to sound economic expansion in Member as well as non-member countries in the process of economic development; and
— to contribute to the expansion of world trade on a multilateral, non-discriminatory basis in accordance with international obligations.

The original Member countries of the OECD are Austria, Belgium, Canada, Denmark, France, Germany, Greece, Iceland, Ireland, Italy, Luxembourg, the Netherlands, Norway, Portugal, Spain, Sweden, Switzerland, Turkey, the United Kingdom and the United States. The following countries became Members subsequently through accession at the dates indicated hereafter: Japan (28th April 1964), Finland (28th January 1969), Australia (7th June 1971) and New Zealand (29th May 1973). The Commission of the European Communities takes part in the work of the OECD (Article 13 of the OECD Convention). Yugoslavia has a special status at OECD (agreement of 28th October 1961).

The Centre for Educational Research and Innovation was created in June 1968 by the Council of the Organisation for Economic Co-operation and Development.

The main objectives of the Centre are as follows:

— *to promote and support the development of research activities in education and undertake such research activities where appropriate;*
— *to promote and support pilot experiments with a view to introducing and testing innovations in the educational system;*
— *to promote the development of co-operation between Member countries in the field of educational research and innovation.*

The Centre functions within the Organisation for Economic Co-operation and Development in accordance with the decisions of the Council of the Organisation, under the authority of the Secretary-General. It is supervised by a Governing Board composed of one national expert in its field of competence from each of the countries participating in its programme of work.

Publié en français sous le titre :
ÉCOLES ET ENTREPRISES :
un nouveau partenariat

FOREWORD

There has recently been a widespread increase in the amount of contact between education and business in OECD countries. Much of this activity has arisen spontaneously rather than as the result of central policy decisions. Yet in many countries, partnerships with business are becoming a central part of the education process; there is a need to understand their collective influence. At the international level, there has so far been little work on this subject.

This report focuses on one aspect of such partnerships: links between schools and businesses. It is the first major attempt to survey such links at the international level. It results from a CERI activity on partnerships under its project "Technological Change and Human Resources Development". This activity brought together a group of experts on partnerships both from private companies and from public organisations – whose members are listed in Annex 2. The group identified many of the issues and trends summarised in this report. It also concluded that both policy-makers and practitioners concerned with partnerships could gain considerably from understanding parallel developments in other countries. The report is thus intended on the one hand for business leaders and government policy-makers, and on the other for the people in schools and companies engaged in the everyday business of making partnerships work.

The report was written by Mr Donald Hirsch of the CERI Secretariat. The case studies are mainly the result of the Secretariat's own assessments on the basis of visits to projects, in addition to secondary literature.

The report is published on the responsibility of the Secretary-General.

ALSO AVAILABLE

Adult Illiteracy and Economic Performance (1992)
(96 91 03 1) ISBN 92-64-13597-9   FF95   £13.00   US$24.00   DM39

Curriculum Reform. An Overview of Trends *by Malcolm Skilbeck* (1990)
(96 90 01 1) ISBN 92-64-13311-9   FF80   £10.00   US$17.00   DM32

Education and the Economy in a Changing Society (1989)
(91 88 03 1) ISBN 92-64-13176-0   FF80   £10.00   US$17.00   DM33

Human Resources and Corporate Strategy. Technological Change in Banks and Insurance Companies: France, Germany, Japan, Sweden, United States *by Olivier Bertrand, Thierry Noyelle* (1988)
(96 88 01 1) ISBN 92-64-13096-9   FF70   £8.50   US$15.50   DM31

TABLE OF CONTENTS

SUMMARY   7

Chapter 1 INTRODUCTION – THE PARTNERSHIP PHENOMENON   9

Working together   10
Partnership types – a brief round-up   11
Understanding partnerships   14

Chapter 2 THE PARTNERSHIP PROCESS – WHAT MAKES IT WORK?   17

Getting introduced   17
Getting acquainted   19
Living together   20
Frictions – and divorce?   21

Chapter 3 THE PARTNERSHIP MISSION: CHANGES IN EDUCATION – AND
BEYOND   23

Partnership for what?   23
Three motives   23
Partnerships in general education: new routes to learning   25
Partnerships in vocational education: schools under fire   29
Partnerships and the transition to work: the compact experiment   32
Partnerships and the teacher: breaking the closed circle   33
Partnerships and the school: exploring new styles   34
A ''bottom line'' for business?   35

Chapter 4 PARTNERSHIPS IN CONTEXT: THE ART OF THE POSSIBLE   41

The national context   41
The economic context   45
The context of scale   46

Chapter 5 CONCLUSION   49

A balanced partnership?   50
Challenger or collaborator?   50
A broader partnership?   51

CASE STUDIES   53

Annex 1: Addresses for further information   105
Annex 2: CERI expert group on education-business partnerships, 1990-1991   109

SUMMARY

The past decade has seen an explosion of new contacts between education and outside individuals and organisations. The main cause has been the perception that education influenced only by the State has had serious shortcomings, in particular in terms of preparing pupils for the workforce.

This report focuses on partnerships between businesses and schools. Such links have multiplied as employers have seen that the best way to influence schools is to work together with them, and schools have realised that they share many goals with employers. There is also a hope that the relationship will influence the behaviour of business, for example by encouraging companies to value and use educated workers more imaginatively. But changes in education have in practice been the dominant objective.

The report looks at two aspects of partnerships: what makes them work well, and what kind of impact they are having on education and on business.

Partnerships tend to involve a gradual building of trust between the two sides. Early on, activities are kept simple and often symbolic. But in the longer term, effective partnerships need to find ways of changing aspects of education *systems,* rather than just running one-off activities. In doing so, the partners often formulate new joint goals based on a common understanding of what needs to change. So partnership is a dynamic process, not just an agreement between two sides with pre-set, fixed objectives.

What are partnerships trying to achieve? Employers have varying reasons for trying to influence education. Some want to raise academic standards, others to give pupils more "relevant" experiences, while others believe that schools need to teach different general skills. Although there is potential for these aims to conflict, they often prove in practice to be complementary.

Some important changes attempted by partnerships have been:
- The development of *new learning styles* in general education, to make pupils into the adaptable and thoughtful workers that employers now need.
- Improvements to *vocational education,* making it more relevant to workplace practice, and rethinking the balance between vocational and general studies.
- The creation of new *links between school and work* – for example through compacts between businesses and schools.
- The broadening of *teachers'* experience of the world outside school.
- The application of private sector wisdom to *school management* styles.
- Changes in *business behaviour,* notably in recruitment and training.

Partnerships have enjoyed greatest influence when they have been a catalyst for existing educational reform movements supported or initiated by governments, rather than when working against the grain. Partly for this reason, the national context has strongly influenced what partnerships have been able to achieve in each OECD country.

The 1980s have shown that partnerships can play an important role at the centre of educational change. To consolidate that position in the 1990s, businesses will have to establish a permanent working relationship with education, yet avoid becoming so institutionalised within the system that they no longer challenge the *status quo*.

Chapter 1

INTRODUCTION – THE PARTNERSHIP PHENOMENON

"I wish to encourage, from lower secondary school onwards, the genuine opening-up of education to the world of business." (Edith Cresson, May 1991, in her first speech to the National Assembly as France's Prime Minister)

This report is about the recent growth in co-operation between schools and businesses in OECD countries. It is about schoolchildren in Milan spending a month working in a company as part of their studies, about teachers in Yorkshire temporarily swapping places with workers from the local cake factory, about a large corporation in Virginia helping to design a new curriculum in a vocational high school. It is also about coalitions and compacts between employers, schools and others that aim at widespread improvement in school systems. The term ''partnership'' is here used as a shorthand to describe this co-operation – referring both to individual projects and to the general collaboration between business and education.

The quotation from the French Prime Minister demonstrates the high political priority now being given to school-business partnerships in many countries. It also contains an important premise on which the commitment to partnership is often based: education has been depicted as an insular activity that needs to allow in outside influences. The past decade has seen an explosion of new contacts between educational bodies and outsiders – particularly employers – aimed at ending this isolation.

The portrayal of education as a cut-off island has always been a caricature. In reality, ever since medieval European schools and universities served the needs of the Christian church by teaching Latin and theology, there have been strong links between education and some of the more powerful forces in society. In the present century, the force that has had overwhelmingly the greatest influence on education has been the State. Until relatively recently, it was tacitly accepted in many countries that the State was a satisfactory vehicle for transmitting society's priorities to the education system.

Now, that consensus has disappeared. There is instead a broad movement to widen the range of organisations and individuals who influence and get involved with education (fashionably referred to as ''stockholders''). This movement is very new in some countries; in others it dates from the 1970s. It has been motivated by a number of perceptions, mainly relating to supposed failures of education systems financed and governed almost entirely by the State. A central concern is that schools have become increasingly out of touch with the knowledge and skills that pupils will require when they start work.

Another worry is that there is too little dialogue with communities and parents about the direction of educational change. Some critics are apt to blame the ''educational establishment'' rather than governments: teachers are accused of being unaccountable for the styles they adopt or the results they produce. But there is a common concern that state bureaucracies have failed to channel effectively the demands on education made by society – and that these demands need urgently to be heeded.

This report looks at one of the ways education has been opening up to outside forces – the creation of partnerships between initial schooling (both general and vocational) and businesses, as well as other employers[1]. It does not cover higher education, and touches only incidentally on partnerships with parents, community groups and other non-business interests. This selectiveness is an attempt to focus analysis within the vast and amorphous subject of education in partnership.

School-business links have been chosen as an area where clear trends are developing in many OECD countries, yet have been little analysed beyond the national context. In contrast, higher education's changing relationship with the private sector has already been documented at the international level[2]. That cannot be said of broader partnerships involving education, business and "the community", which are likely to be significant in the 1990s. But during the 1980s, and still today, schools have looked more than anywhere else to the world of work as a means of improving their contact with outsiders. School-business partnerships have now been around for long enough in some countries to offer valuable lessons for those embarking on similar ventures elsewhere.

Working together

The proliferation of partnerships between business and education derives more than anything else from a remarkable new willingness for the two to work together, shedding a long-standing mutual suspicion. Yet, the new interest of employers in education derives largely from an analysis of education's failures under state domination. How, then, can business involvement in education be described as a partnership, as opposed to an attempted take-over? This is an important question that hangs over most school-business relationships.

There are few if any cases of genuine business take-over of education. True, there are instances of schools set up with substantial corporate support, and hence subject to strong corporate influence. The United Kingdom's City Technology Colleges and America's corporate academies were both founded with contributions from big business, which has affected the shape of the curriculum in these schools, as well as their ethos. But even in these cases there has been neither a radical departure from existing teaching methods or school structures, nor an attempt by business to wrest the day-to-day management of schools from educators. These cases illustrate the first answer to the question posed above: whatever its critique of education, business does not have the expertise to impose alternatives on its own, and knows that change must involve co-operation with professional educators.

The second answer relates to the attitude of the educators. Their legendary hostility to business, if it ever existed, has been greatly modified in recent years. There are several factors contributing to this change. The simplest is political mood: capitalism and enterprise, having been out of fashion in the 1960s, became respectable again in the 1980s. But in the case of teachers, the 1980s brought the added reason of unemployment for sympathising with business priorities, and indeed with employers' critique of education's shortcomings. Teachers in many OECD countries have seen large proportions of their pupils failing to get jobs when they left school. That has encouraged them both to listen harder to what employers want and to look for closer links between school and the workplace.

As teachers started to get involved in partnerships, they discovered another important reason for shedding their suspicion of business. The objectives of the two partners were often far more similar than either had imagined. There has long been assumed an inherent conflict between the narrow aim of preparing a child for work and the lofty objective of cultivating his or her mind. Insofar as companies need recruits with technical skills related to specific tasks, that conflict remains a real one.

But, increasingly, the most important skills needed at work, and those that firms want to encourage schools to teach, are more general. Thinking flexibly, communicating well, working well in teams, using initiative – these and other ''generic'' skills in the workforce are becoming crucial to firms' competitiveness[3]. This trend fits well with independent changes in the philosophy of teaching. Many teachers have been trying to move away from the tradition of primarily transmitting knowledge to their pupils, and instead want to teach them to think and learn for themselves. Happily for such teachers and their pupils, initiative and decision-taking in the schoolroom turns out to be excellent preparation for the modern workplace. It is true that not all teachers are inclined to put greater emphasis on such skills, just as many companies are not yet good at making use of them. But companies with the most sophisticated human resource policies are often pulling in much the same direction as schools with the most innovative programmes of curriculum development.

A further reason for a new co-operative spirit is that businesses have an increasingly strong direct interest in maintaining friendly links with schools. As the population of school-leaving cohorts in most OECD countries dwindles, companies are having to compete for young workers. They are starting to realise the importance of establishing contact with potential recruits while they are still at school.

Finally, a new willingness to work together is made more likely where businesses, as well as schools, are ready to change their behaviour. Teachers are understandably reluctant to listen to business leaders apparently telling them how to do their job if they feel that employers will not listen, for example, to complaints about hiring practices that do not do justice to particular young people's abilities. Some businesses are now willing to see partnerships as more than just a way to change education. They are prepared to consider changing some of their own practices, especially where they believe that this will help them to recruit young people. Nevertheless, the great majority of partnerships involving schools still concentrate on educational change, and that asymmetry is reflected in the subject matter of this report.

Partnership types – a brief round-up

What forms of partnership have emerged as a result of this new understanding? Many. It is impossible to produce any comprehensive list of forms of co-operation occurring in OECD countries, or even to slot partnerships into any neat classification. There are various elements common to many partnerships, but each project is unique in the way it combines them, and relates them to local circumstances. The case studies described at the end of this report give 24 examples. But before proceeding with this

Figure 1.1. **School-industry links, England, June 1989**
Most common activities

Secondary schools with:

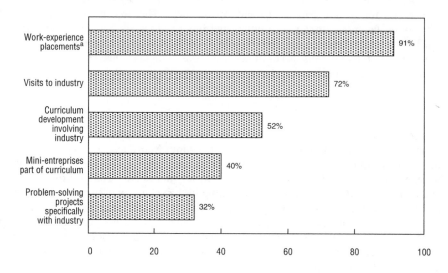

Primary schools with:

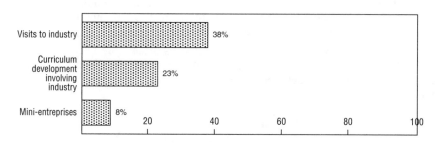

a. In schools which had pupils in their final compulsory year
Source : Department of Education and Science, *Statistical Bulletin 10/90*, London, 1990.

analysis of the partnership phenomenon, it is worth briefly mentioning some of the most commonly encountered features.

There is little reliable data on this diffuse phenomenon. But one certainty is that the vast majority of partnerships are small, local and basic. In the United Kingdom and the United States, where partnerships have been studied in more detail than in most other countries, surveys give some approximation of the pattern of activity. Two examples are shown in Figures 1.1 and 1.2. These results are strongly influenced by the categories selected for the surveys. But they do give an indication of the extent of partnership: the American survey identified projects in a majority of the country's school districts; the British one found that some 90 per cent of secondary schools and 54 per cent of primary schools had links with industry.

Most projects involve simple forms of co-operation between a company and a school. *Work-experience placements* are the most common activity in the United Kingdom as in many European countries, if only because these are often required by governments. In France, for example, the *séquences éducatives en entreprise* have been a standard feature of vocational high schools since the late 1970s. Reinforcing this link with the workplace, *visits to companies* by pupils and teachers, *work shadowing* (observation of a worker's daily routine) and *teacher secondment* have become increasingly popular. But much activity also goes on within schools, notably *curriculum development* projects, and the establishment of *mini-enterprises.* In the United States, significant

Figure 1.2. **Partnership analysis by type of objective**
United-States

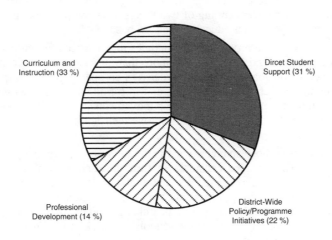

Curriculum and Instruction (33 %)

Dircet Student Support (31 %)

Professional Development (14 %)

District-Wide Policy/Programme Initiatives (22 %)

Source: National Association of Partners in Education, Alexandra, Virginia.

emphasis has been given to direct help from companies to schools and students – such as one-to-one *mentorships* of pupils by company employees, *"adopt-a-school"* initiatives and *donation of equipment.*

Partnerships that go beyond specific activity based on a company's relationship with a school are harder to classify. *Coalitions* have been set up to change education in a variety of ways. The most coherent model is the *compact,* where employers in an area agree to give jobs to pupils who meet certain educational objectives – but even this form has a number of variations. More one-sided *business coalitions* have been common in North America; their *lobbying* of government bodies for improvements in schooling perhaps does not count as partnerships. But big companies are becoming more action-oriented, and inclined to launch their own *programmes that reward innovation* across an entire school system.

Other coalitions are based around programmes originated by public, semi-public or other non-profit bodies. Such schemes may aim, for example, to *promote enterprise* in schools, *improve career guidance,* or *retrain teachers* with business co-operation. Such programmes, and partnerships in general, tend to be concentrated on *upper secondary schooling,* and designed in particular for pupils engaged in *vocational and pre-vocational studies.* In other words, there is a tendency for public authorities as well as many businesses to direct partnership efforts towards pupils close to making the transition from school to work.

Understanding partnerships

All the partnership types referred to above appear to work well as individual projects, and invariably have positive results in the eyes of their participants. Some reports on partnerships consist largely of emphasizing the value of the various efforts that are being made – perhaps a necessary process as part of the building of a consensus that accepts business's new role in education. This report attempts to move beyond mere praise, towards a better understanding of two things: how the partnership process works, and what its final impact is on education and on business.

Chapter 2 looks at the process, and concludes that a successful partnership between business and education tends to consist of more than just an instant agreement between two sides with common goals. Rather, the process of co-operation is itself important, both in building confidence between the partners and in formulating common goals. Thus, as partnerships mature, and indeed as partnership movements in individual countries mature, they change in character and content, and improve their ability to bring about significant change in education.

Chapter 3 looks at those changes: what is the mission of partnerships, and how well can they deliver? This chapter considers in turn the main aspects of education that partnerships have attempted to change. Its central conclusion is that partnerships succeed best where they go with the grain of initiatives being taken within public schooling systems: they can be a useful catalyst for such change. Where they go against the grain, or where instruments for reforming public schools are weak, it is difficult for partnership schemes to change systems on their own.

For that reason, the context of national school systems are essential in determining what kind of partnerships are possible – as are other cultural factors specific to countries.

Chapter 4 examines some of these cultural factors, and how they help explain different patterns of partnership activity. But while these factors set important constraints, they do not prevent countries from learning important lessons from one another. This chapter also looks at two other background factors that affect partnerships – the state of the national economy and the character of a local community.

The report concludes in Chapter 5 that partnerships can and will play an important part at the centre of change in education during the years to come. The variety of initiatives is a great strength, but for partnerships to consolidate their role over the long term they will have to be more than a series of random contacts whose main impact is to make their participants feel good. The challenge for business will be to maintain enthusiasm and the fresh eye of the outsider to education, while becoming a regular part of the process of mainstream educational change.

NOTES

1. There is a tendency to use the words "business" and "employers" interchangeably. The purpose of this report is to look at links between schools and various public and private enterprises, hitherto referred to for short as "businesses", or collectively as "business". The word "employer" will be used only to refer to an organisation specifically as a hirer of labour.

2. *Industry and University – New Forms of Co-operation and Communication,* Paris: OECD, 1984. This publication is updated by "University-Enterprise Relations in OECD Member Countries", an unpublished report to the OECD's Committee for Scientific and Technological Policy, 1990.

3. See for example *Human Resources and Corporate Strategy: Technological Change in Banks and Insurance Companies,* Paris: OECD/CERI, 1988, Chapter 4; "New Technology and Human Resource Development in the Automobile Industry", Paris: OECD/CERI (document for general distribution), 1986.

Chapter 2

THE PARTNERSHIP PROCESS – WHAT MAKES IT WORK?

"Most successful partnerships depend on strong leadership from the top by an irrationally committed individual." (Gail Niedernhofer, Director for Corporate and Community Liaison, Office of the United States Secretary of Education)

Education-business partnerships are full of missionaries. Their mission is to open up a channel of communication and co-operation which has hitherto been closed. Overcoming the barrier that has existed between business and schools is not, in their view, a routine process. It involves winning hearts and minds – at every level from education minister to teacher, from chief executive to junior employee – to a new way of doing things.

Because this task is so different in nature from the routine activities of both business and education, there has been much attention given to the process of building partnerships. Indeed, the importance attached to disseminating workable partnership models explains the existence of a Corporate and Community Liaison unit within the office of the United States Secretary of Education.

The diversity of partnerships and their objectives makes it impossible to describe any single pattern, or set of criteria for success. Yet there are certain features that recur with remarkable frequency across a variety of projects. Perhaps the most important general feature is that partnerships evolve with time, rather than being executed in a single stage according to unchanging criteria and objectives. A partnership is a moving picture, not a still photograph. This chapter is guided by that dynamic aspect. It looks in turn at the initial idea of co-operation, at the early stages of a partnership in which partners gain each other's confidence, at the way in which those initial contacts transform into a mature relationship and at the potential for that relationship coming under strain.

Getting introduced

Nowhere is the inspiration and commitment of individuals more important than at the very beginning of the partnership process, when somebody has an idea and has to persuade others to co-operate. In several of the case studies carried out for this report, the initial influence of an individual was particularly important: the founder and owner of an Austrian metalworks willing to pay for a new kind of schooling for local children (case study 10); a superintendent in Santa Fe, New Mexico dedicated to restructuring the city's schools (case study 14); a French school inspector with a vision of how pupils could learn through the setting up of small companies (case study 4). In each of these cases, the individual's vision was crucial to get the project up and running. But in each case the project has survived the departure of that individual, who took care to build mechanisms in which he was ultimately dispensable. In other cases, however, the "political will" behind a programme has waned on the departure of the main individuals behind it: that happened after the transfer of the school superintendent who inaugurated the Boston Compact, according to one commentary[1].

Thus, initiative most commonly comes from one person or group, either from business or from education. But there are also some cases in which a coincidence of timing produces a genuinely joint initiative. For example when Digital Equipment in Scotland was trying to formulate a new education strategy, the public authorities in the area were looking for ways of enhancing links with industry; an interesting enterprise simulation exercise resulted (case study 1).

Does it matter whether the "first move" comes from education or from business? Not necessarily: once a project is conceived, there may be equal input from both sides. Frequently, however, the lead continues to be taken by one of the partners. The majority of the case-study examples from Continental Europe in this report result from initiatives taken by schools or public education authorities, where business has played a supporting role. These projects largely involve attempts to improve vocational education; the contribution of business is highly valued, but objectives continue to be set mainly by educators and public administrators.

In the United States, on the other hand, big business has increasingly been showing a willingness to take the initiative. A recent high-profile example is RJR Nabisco's commitment to give $30 million over five years in grants to "Next Century Schools" that come up with radical proposals to improve education. More ambitious still is the New American Schools Development Corporation, set up in July 1991 by prominent chief executives, which aims to raise $150 million to $200 million of private money to improve American education. Teams will be commissioned to design, implement and disseminate new practices. In both these programmes the initiative will remain with the private sector to the extent that boards appointed by business will judge the merits of various projects. But since the aim is to take the best ideas from within education, mustering existing expertise, educators will play at least an equal role in the partnership. That has certainly been the experience with the Panasonic Foundation (see case study 14), which uses corporate funding to help educators spread their own best practice.

But initiative from business can mean more than just big corporations sponsoring educational innovation. Smaller firms are more inclined to address a perceived need in local schools through direct involvement (see for example case studies 10 and 13). Many large companies are also trying to develop a balanced partnership with education through regular co-operation between their local sites and surrounding schools.

Most of the United Kingdom's largest companies now have a scheme systematising school links. The earliest major company initiative of this type was British Petroleum's School Link Scheme. Dating from the 1960s, it is a model which has influenced many others. The system is straightforward: BP sites look for ways they can co-operate with local schools, using "link officers" at each site and "link teachers" at each school to establish a dialogue. They set up activities of mutual benefit, ranging from work shadowing to industrial help with curriculum development to the provision of information on education trends for industrialists. One important aspect of this approach is that although

18

BP has taken the initiative at the national level, it has set up mechanisms which allow schools with their own ideas to make use of the scheme. In fact, in countries like the United Kingdom where there are so many overlapping initiatives, any one scheme often has several labels attached to it. When initiative is coming from several directions, the risk of any one partner dominating is reduced.

Getting acquainted

The early months or years of any partnership may be strongly influenced by the fact that the partners still feel strange in each other's company. The emphasis in this period is often on promoting contacts, however simple, which make partners feel good about each other. A business may decide to "adopt a school", perhaps donating money for specific items such as computers, or encouraging its employees to talk to classes about the firm's work. Teachers may seek out opportunities for visits to a factory, for themselves or for their pupils. Much stress is often put on creating a bond between a specific company and a specific school – such as in the French *jumelages* (twinnings). At this stage, there may be no concerted attempt to use partnerships to change the methods or content of education.

Such links without tangible educational benefit have been dubbed "feel-good partnerships". It is easy to see that term as derogatory. A company that gives a grant to its local school may feel a warm glow (as well as an improvement of its public image), despite having made only a superficial contribution to education. A teacher who invites the managing director of the local sausage factory to address her social science class may feel she is making school more relevant, even though the talk has no impact on the rest of her teaching.

In cases where partnerships never move beyond this "feel-good" stage, it is valid to question their long-term value. A complaint particularly common recently in the United States is that there have been plenty of symbolic links between education and business, but few that attempt to reform fundamentally a school system widely perceived to be failing. (That worry helps explain the reformist goals of the New American Schools Development Corporation, described above.) Certainly the balance portrayed in the survey of American partnerships described in Chapter 1 seems to confirm a preponderance of links that attempt to compensate for the present system rather than change it – such as mentorships, where children in difficulty are given moral and other support by a firm's employees. In the long term there is a danger that "feel-good" partnerships will turn sour, if the inadequacies in education that prompted business involvement do not appear to have been remedied.

Yet the importance of "feel-good" partnerships should not be under-rated, especially in cultures where schools start out nervous of contact with business – fearing, for example, that employers may try to hijack the curriculum for their own purposes. In countries like France and Italy, where the national government keeps a tight control over virtually every aspect of education, outsiders have been kept well away from classrooms. Although this is starting to change, there remains widespread resistance to involving business in certain areas – for example in devising the curriculum. In such circumstances, any thoroughgoing partnership between business and education to improve schools needs to be preceded by a period of learning to work together.

One common aspect of this early stage is that the partners may be using the project for their own narrow purposes. A school seeking on-the-job experience for final-year students to match new educational priorities may find a work-experience placement with a firm whose main aim is to get a "free look" at next year's potential recruits. A chemical company may send an employee to talk to a geography class, as part of an effort to improve the "dirty" image of the industry; the teacher's purpose may be to improve pupils' understanding of industrial and economic activity.

But in the process of this contact, common purposes may be discovered. In the chemical company example, the employee may discover that a broader project on eco-nomic awareness, related to his industry, would be of mutual interest. The teacher, initially sceptical of subjecting children to propaganda about the chemical industry, may find that the firm can supply materials to support an existing geography project on the environment. As co-operation increases, both sides could realise that they have a com-mon interest in encouraging children to solve problems in groups rather than only relating to the teacher as individuals. Gradually, in other words, a marriage of convenience can start to change into one in which goals and values are shared.

Living together

The most enthusiastic pioneers of the partnership "movement" have a vision of an ideal form of business co-operation with education. This paradigm involves a *coalition* of those in a community who are most concerned with education – businesses, educational organisations and other groups and individuals – working together in *commonly-agreed directions* for change in the school *system, and beyond*[2]. Such an ideal is rarely if ever achieved in quite that form, but contains a number of elements that distinguish a cosy arrangement between a school and a company from something more influential.

Coalitions extend partnerships beyond a simple school-business link. As well as bringing together a number of businesses and schools, they may also bring in others with an interest in education. Two examples of broad coalitions, both from Canada, appear in the case studies (case 21, in Ottawa, and case 23, in Toronto). Their breadth can bring important benefits. In the Toronto case, the coalition organised a dazzling network of mutually beneficial learning activities throughout the district. Thus, for example, people learning craft skills in a carpentry workshop made furniture for a day-care centre where students in child care looked after the small children of teenage mothers to allow them to complete high school. In the Ottawa case, the advantage lay in bringing together all responsible authorities to facilitate change: for example, an exchange scheme between teachers and engineers was authorised despite the fact that the engineers lacked the necessary teaching licenses.

A potential drawback of broad coalitions is that they can become unfocused. Thus, the most successful ones are generally "umbrella schemes" which help co-ordinate a number of more specific initiatives. There is also a danger that many overlapping initiatives can cause confusion among schools and businesses wishing to get involved. In the United Kingdom there have been complaints along these lines, which to some extent have been dealt with by a rationalisation of programmes – for example in the merger of schemes that are complementary (see case study 3 – "Evolution" and "Comment").

Commonly-agreed directions can bring about more effective change than when the partners are pursuing their own goals. The development of common goals in the early stages of partnerships has been referred to above. Many businesses first enter into partnerships with some firm ideas about what is wrong with education, but only vague notions of how to put it right. In the early stages, they pick up from educators a better understanding of how new learning styles can improve things, and of how they can make a distinctive contribution. This was clearly so in both case studies on school-run mini-enterprises – one in the United Kingdom (case 3) and the other in France (case 4). In these cases the industrial partner – a national bank and a local Chamber of Commerce, respectively – were initially motivated by a general desire to "do something" to help education. As they got involved, they began to understand and contribute to the educational value of mini-enterprises, while finding ways of using employee involvement to the best advantage of the project.

System change can be clearly distinguished from change which applies only within the limits of a particular project. Do partnerships offer merely new activities, or new ways of doing things? Movement towards the latter is perhaps the most important way in which the impact of partnerships can grow. The ways in which partnerships aim to have an impact on education systems are discussed in Chapter 3.

Here it is worth noting that it can be difficult for partnership projects on their own to produce general change in educational methods. Renault's new technological resource centre in Billancourt, near Paris (case study 7), offers students in vocational schools the opportunity to spend a week of learning with state-of-the-art technology; that is an activity with specific benefit. Its sponsors hope that it will also help improve learning styles in vocational schools; that would be a system change. So far, however, teachers and students appear to regard the resource centre as incidental to their main curriculum, which is centrally regulated by the State. Despite the involvement of the education authorities, an initiative sited at a private company does not yet seem to have been synchronised with change taking place inside classrooms. That may change as the scheme develops.

Schools and beyond. A final aspect of some maturing partnerships is that participants start asking whether the main aim should always be improvements in education. Of course, every partnership has some benefit for all parties – otherwise they would not participate. But the emphasis tends to be on the benefits available to everyone from a better education system. In a few cases, however, partners are exploring how education can return the favour and help business or the community. At least one partnership has tried to turn the concept of "adopt-a-school" on its head, with an "adopt-an-industry" scheme. The scope for such mutual help may often be limited; examples are discussed in the final section of Chapter 3. But there is no doubt that where direct benefits can be spread beyond the school, partnerships will become stronger and more durable. Arrangements based on semi-altruistic behaviour of firms with a general interest in "improving education" are vulnerable – to changes in the prevailing mood, and to economic recession.

Frictions – and divorce?

Could the fashion for public-private co-operation that affected most OECD countries in the 1980s be reversed? It seems unlikely that businesses could be totally evicted from schools, although they might reduce their involvement of their own accord if their perception of their interests changed. But there will continue to be some aspects of cultural difference that potentially make the relationship between business and schools an uneasy one.

The most obvious difference is that businesses are profit-making organisations with "bottom lines" and shareholders, while education is a social activity whose results are assessed according to a range of non-financial criteria. There are signs that the 1990s might see a narrowing of this aspect of cultural difference. Firms are increasingly pursuing objectives that do not directly relate to financial results, if only because social responsibility (for example towards the environment) is becoming more important to their customers. At the same time, education is becoming more inclined to define some bottom line of results (again under pressure from its customers), and also to relate those results to the economy and employment.

But an important remaining friction is a difference in time horizons. A secondary school with six or seven age groups needs to look nearly a decade ahead when planning some change that will affect a pupil from entry up to graduation. Most companies are used to looking for quick results, and find it hard to commit resources over very long periods. Change of personnel, merger or budget squeeze can potentially transform the company's outlook towards partnerships. It must be noted however that in the course of this study, little evidence was found of fickleness on the part of companies. Once involved in partnerships, businesses have on the whole demonstrated loyalty and enthusiasm for the educational causes espoused. But over the coming years, as the novelty of partnership wears off and fashions change, that loyalty may face new tests.

NOTES

1. Eleanor Farrar, *The Boston Compact – A Teaching Case,* New Brunswick, New Jersey: Center for Policy Research in Education, Rutgers, 1988, pp.35-37.
2. This, roughly, was the paradigm arrived at by the OECD/CERI expert group on business-education partnerships whose meetings contributed to this report. Its members, however, were keen to emphasize that partnerships meeting some or all of these criteria are not inherently more valuable than those that do not. Rather, the paradigm represents the directions in which mature partnerships tend to evolve, potentially widening their influence.

Chapter 3

THE PARTNERSHIP MISSION: CHANGES
IN EDUCATION – AND BEYOND

"Schools seeking to deliver a broad, balanced, work-related curriculum for their pupils have increasingly looked to employers... Education partnership isn't any longer an optional extra for employers, but a mainstream business necessity."
(George Simpson, Chief Executive, Rover Group)

Partnership for what?

Many advocates of business-education partnership see it as a worthwhile goal in itself. Schools are encouraged to open themselves up to outside influences, businesses to get involved in education; such co-operation, it is assumed, will be good for them both. Organisations promoting partnerships give ideas of how to start a project, stress the importance of having a clear "business plan", of evaluating results, and so on. In other words, there is much interest in the partnership process. Sometimes it is possible to lose sight of a more fundamental question: what are partnerships trying to achieve?

This chapter reviews some of the problems that partnerships have most commonly attempted to tackle in OECD countries. It starts by distinguishing three broad motives for business involvement in education, and considers how these help shape partnerships. It then looks at the type of intervention that has taken place in three successive areas: general education, vocational education and the transition from school to work. Next, it considers how partnerships affect the teaching profession, and the way schools are run. Finally, the chapter discusses the various ways in which partnerships affect businesses.

Three motives

It was noted at the beginning of this report that partnerships stem from the perceived failings of an education system governed and financed almost entirely by the State. But what are these failings? More specifically, what are the shortfalls that make employers believe they are not getting the workers they require?

One common criticism is that education is cocooned in its own closed world, rarely considering the relevance of its output to the needs of the workforce. For example, schools have been accused of giving too much status to academic rather than vocational

23

studies, and also of running vocational programmes that are out of touch with the changing skill needs of industry. This *"relevance" motive* stimulates schemes to give learners greater experience of the wider world, brings greater knowledge of that world into the curriculum and attempts to strengthen vocational schooling through closer links with practitioners.

A distinctly different source of concern is the perception by business in some countries that educational standards have been falling at a time when they need to rise. Even those who dispute this decline would generally not deny that economies require a greater proportion of soundly-educated workers than ever before, or that education systems still fall far short of providing them. Thus the *"standards" motive* causes employers to seek general improvements in education, for example by adding their voices to calls for education reform or lobbying for extra resources. It also gives rise to schemes designed to help improve the teaching of specific academic subjects – most commonly science and mathematics – which too few workers are thought to have mastered.

But improved standards may require more than just extra resources and more time spent on certain subjects. The standards debate also raises the question of educational method and style. There are in some countries strong pressures to reinstate traditional means of instilling literacy and numeracy skills and civic knowledge. However, a further motive for employer concern points in a different direction. This stems from the changing nature of work and the skills required for it. Both the growth in the service sector and the technological transformation of manufacturing have created the need for more workers capable of initiative, thought, and group co-operation, and fewer mere order-takers[1]. But employers fear that education's workforce-related aims are fossilised, and that without a push, schools and colleges will go on teaching as if their students were destined for old-fashioned production lines. This *"skills" motive*[2] is another powerful focus for partnerships – and the one that probably creates the greatest challenges. For it requires employers to do more than just give students a taste of the working world, or support schemes to raise school standards. It requires them to confront the issue of pedagogy, the most jealously guarded prerogative of the professional educator.

In the United States, a commission of business and education leaders brought together by the Secretary of Labor has recently published a first report attempting to define "what work requires of schools"[3]. This body, the Secretary's Commission on Achieving Necessary Skills (SCANS), identifies five "competencies" needed in the workplace and a three-part "foundation" of intellectual skills and personal qualities on which they are based. Listed in Table 3.1, these competences, skills and personal qualities are typical of those recently identified as important by employers in OECD countries. The commission makes two observations – particularly significant for the next stage of its work – on how to ensure that schools actually teach the skills identified in the report. The first is that the present school system does not reflect the balance prescribed in the SCANS list. There is much emphasis on reading and writing, for example; far less on talking and listening. The second is that even basic reading, writing and mathematical skills will have to be approached differently: workers will have to be able to read manuals and understand spreadsheets, not just read textbooks and understand algebra.

Elements of all three motives identified above – relevance, standards and skills – can be found in speeches of company chief executives calling for a new partnership between business and education. Do these motives reinforce or contradict each other? There is scope for both.

Potentially the starkest contradiction is between reinforcing traditional standards and teaching "new" skills. Employers in many countries complain that schools these days are turning out many young adults with poor reading, spelling or numerical abilities. The (largely unproven) perception that standards in these areas have declined is sometimes blamed on modern teaching methods, and schools are under some pressure to return to instilling "the basics" in a form that can be easily tested. Yet certain aspects of newer teaching styles appear to correspond with employers' desire for new skills and relevance: the encouragement of pupils to learn as inquirers rather than just listening to a teacher-lecturer, an emphasis on learning through application rather than simply memorising a body of abstract knowledge, the growing role of "project work", and so on.

There is also a potential conflict – or at least competition – between the "relevance" and "skills" motives. Many partnerships focus on bringing pupils and teachers into contact with the working world, or on improving the relevance of vocational courses. An exercise such as work-shadowing might make a pupil understand more what work is about, but will not on its own improve his or her ability to work in groups, to take responsibility, or to communicate effectively. Nor, necessarily, will specific vocational studies. These "generic" skills might more effectively be developed through new approaches in general education than by increasing direct links between education and work. But there is a strong tendency for partnerships to concentrate on the latter.

In practice, the most imaginative partnerships find ways of combining relevance and the development of new skills. A visit to a factory may serve to demonstrate to teachers and pupils the importance of teamwork; a subsequent classroom project assisted by one of the factory managers may help build teamwork into some everyday learning activity. When industrialists first talk about making education more "relevant", they may think largely in terms of learning about work and industry. As contact with education increases, the concept broadens, to learning in ways that are *apt* to pupils' futures in the workforce, without necessarily having a direct link. Perhaps, therefore, the much-used term of "relevance" might be replaced by "aptness".

Similarly, the movement to raise standards can in practice complement rather than undermine efforts to bring education into line with the requirements of a modern workforce. Employers who get involved with projects to improve science and mathematics have been quick to pick up on successful modern teaching methods rather than insisting on a "traditional" style. When business was more remote from education, some of its leaders tended to join demands for a return to a style of teaching and testing that they could understand in relation to their own school days a generation earlier. A great benefit of partnership is that as business improves its understanding of modern educational methods and certification, its objectives become more sophisticated.

Partnerships in general education: new routes to learning

The greatest challenge that arises from these objectives is to find ways of recasting basic schooling, to improve its ability to prepare young minds for a modern workforce. Secondary schooling in particular does not appear to be producing the well-motivated and well-rounded young people that employers would like to recruit – on the contrary, its effect sometimes seems to be to demotivate them and narrow their perspectives. It is very difficult for vocational education, higher education or adult education to correct for attitudes created during secondary schooling. So partnership between businesses and secondary schools is crucial.

Table 3.1. "What Work Requires of Schools" – An American Definition

---

FIVE COMPETENCIES

Resources: Identifies, organises, plans and allocates resources

A. *Time* – selects goal-relevant activities, ranks them, allocates time, and prepares and follows schedules.
B. *Money* – uses or prepares budgets, makes forecasts, keeps records, and makes adjustments to meet objectives.
C. *Material and facilities* – acquires, stores, allocates, and uses materials or space efficiently.
D. *Human resources* – assesses skills and distributes work accordingly, evaluates performance and provides feedback.

Interpersonal: Works with others

A. *Participates as member of a team* – contributes to group effort.
B. *Teaches others new skills.*
C. *Serves clients/customers* – works to satisfy customers' expectations.
D. *Exercises leadership* – communicates ideas to justify position, persuades and convinces others, responsibly challenges existing procedures and policies.
E. *Negotiates* – works toward agreements involving exchange of resources, resolves divergent interests.
F. *Works with diversity* – works well with men and women from diverse backgrounds.

Information: Acquires and uses information

A. *Acquires and evaluates information.*
B. *Organises and maintains information.*
C. *Interprets and communicates information.*
D. *Uses computers to process information.*

Systems: Understands complex inter-relationships

A. *Understands systems* – knows how social, organisational, and technological systems work, and operates effectively with them.
B. *Monitors and corrects performance* – distinguishes trends, predicts impacts on system operations, diagnoses deviations in systems' performance and corrects malfunctions.
C. *Improves or designs systems* – suggests modifications to existing systems and develops new or alternative systems to improve performance.

Technology: Works with a variety of technologies

A. *Selects technology* – chooses procedures, tools or equipment, including computers and related technologies.
B. *Applies technology to task* – understands overall intent and proper procedures for set-up and operation of equipment.
C. *Maintains and troubleshoots equipment* – prevents, identifies, or solves problems with equipment, including computers and other technologies.

Basic skills: Reads, writes, performs arithmetic and mathematical operations, listens and speaks

A.   *Reading* – locates, understands, and interprets written information in prose and in documents such as manuals, graphs, and schedules.
B.   *Writing* – communicates thoughts, ideas, information and messages in writing and creates documents such as letters, directions, manuals, reports, graphs and flow charts.
C.   *Arithmetic/mathematics* – performs basic computations and approaches practical problems by choosing appropriately from a variety of mathematical techniques.
D.   *Listening* – receives, attends to, interprets, and responds to verbal messages and other cues.
E.   *Speaking* – organises ideas and communicates orally.

Thinking skills: Thinks creatively, makes decisions, solves problems, visualises, knows how to learn and reasons

A.   *Creative thinking* – generates new ideas.
B.   *Decision-making* – specifies goals and constraints, generates alternatives, considers risks, and evaluates and chooses best alternative.
C.   *Problem-solving* – recognises problems and devises and implements plan of action.
D.   *Seeing things in the mind's eye* – organises and processes symbols, pictures, graphs, objects and other information.
E.   *Knowing how to learn* – uses efficient learning techniques to acquire and apply new knowledge and skills.
F.   *Reasoning* – discovers a rule or principle underlying the relationship between two or more objects and applies it in solving a problem.

Personal qualities: Displays responsibility, self-esteem, sociability, self-management, and integrity and honesty

A.   *Responsibility* – exerts a high level of effort and perseveres towards goal attainment.
B.   *Self-esteem* – believes in own self-worth and maintains a positive view of self.
C.   *Sociability* – demonstrates understanding, friendliness, adaptability, empathy, and politeness in group settings.
D.   *Self-management* – assesses self accurately, sets personal goals, monitors progress, and exhibits self-control.
E.   *Integrity/honesty* – chooses ethical courses of action.

Source: Secretary's Commission on Achieving Necessary Skills, *What Work Requires of Schools*, Washington, D.C.: Department of Labor, 1991.

A distinction has already been noted between schemes that simply inform secondary school pupils about the world of work and those that attempt to help change the ways in which they learn. Certainly the first type of scheme is more straightforward to organise, while the second risks friction as people from outside education appear to be telling teachers how to do their jobs. But in practice, there have been many successful examples of companies working together with teachers towards a common vision of new learning styles. Perhaps the most helpful concept defining the direction of such initiatives is "enterprise learning".

The potential role of enterprise in today's education and training systems is explored in a recent monograph prepared for the OECD/CERI[4]. The author defines a set of "enterprise skills" as, broadly:

"...those personal dispositions, abilities and competences related to creativity, initiative, problem-solving, flexibility, adaptability, the taking and discharging of responsibility and knowing how to learn and relearn." (p. 10)

These are the skills that are needed at a time of "unprecedented and unpredictable change", it is argued. Adaptability is needed to cope with future changes, while a new style of work organisation requires workers with the other skills listed.

The role of enterprise in education is frequently misunderstood. "Enterprise learning" does not just mean learning *about* enterprise, but learning *through* enterprise, as well as learning to be enterprising. And as the definition above shows, learning to be enterprising does not have to mean learning to be an entrepreneur, in the commercial sense. An enterprise can be any form of undertaking or project, not just a business one.

A distinction can also be made between educational projects based specifically on the creation and running of an enterprise, and those that choose other methods of teaching enterprising skills. Thus "mini-enterprises" in schools are a useful way of teaching children to take initiative and to work together, though not the only way. Some business simulations in schools are designed specifically to nurture potential entrepreneurs (see for example "Outcomes" in case study 9). Others are used as vehicles for teaching other things – how to work with fellow-students for a common purpose, how to manage a budget, how to plan effectively, and so on (case studies 3 and 4). The British scheme (case 3) has evolved from an initiative designed mainly to create new entrepreneurs into a project aimed at developing enterprise across the curriculum.

Companies involved in partnerships with schools have found real or simulated business exercises a useful means of lending their own expertise to educationally desirable activity. Whether they involve setting up and running a company for a year, or just spending a half-day designing a new lay-out for an office or classroom, such projects tend to have several common features. One is that they are good at motivating pupils, even those not motivated by their regular studies. An important reason is that they require pupils to solve problems in groups, rather than simply asking individuals to answer questions for which there is a pre-set answer. Another feature is that such exercises cut across the compartmentalisation of time and subject matter (into single-subject, 50-minute lessons) conventional in secondary schools – allowing more continuity and connection between various elements of learning. Such aspects of partnership projects can potentially be applied more generally in a school's curriculum.

"Whilst 'entrepreneurship' can be packaged as a curriculum product", notes the OECD monograph (p. 39)[4], "it would appear to be less possible when it comes to the broader approach to enterprise, which is a process, not a product." Thus, the "enterprise skills" defined above may be encouraged by any given project, but need also to be incorporated into a general approach to teaching. For this reason, partnerships have been most successful in influencing secondary education when two conditions apply. The first is that their goals correspond to reform initiatives taking place from within the public education system. The second is that contact between a school and businesses is not limited to a single project but takes place at several levels – involving pupils and their teachers, inside and away from school, across a range of subject disciplines.

A good example of where both of the above conditions are met is under the United Kingdom's Technical and Vocational Education Initiative (TVEI). Launched in 1983 as a pilot scheme and made available everywhere in the country by 1992, this programme aims to cultivate a new approach to education for 14-18 year-olds. The components of the programme vary from one school to another, but everywhere it aims to multiply links with business, to bring adults from outside school into classrooms, to develop a new style of teaching and to promote "economic and industrial understanding". The influence of TVEI on secondary schooling in the United Kingdom is pervasive, and every British partnership described in this report has some link with it (see especially case studies 18 and 19). By developing common approaches to change in upper secondary schooling – which are in principle reflected in the new national curriculum – TVEI ensures that each new partnership builds on existing trends.

Partnerships in vocational education: schools under fire

Two central issues underlie recent debates on vocational education. The first is how much of it should be provided, and to whom. The second is how it should be delivered: what should be the respective roles of schools and employers? At the heart of both issues is the problem of how to prepare employees for the growing number of occupations where workers need to combine technical competence with a high level of numerical, communication and thinking skills.

The amount of vocational education offered in the latter part of secondary schooling varies enormously among OECD countries, as does the number of pupils who get any at all. One factor that can limit demand for vocational education is that it is commonly seen as a low-status option, taken mainly by those pupils who are not capable of benefiting from a purely academic curriculum. It may be impossible, for cultural reasons, ever to remove this bias entirely in most countries. But the bias is weaker in places (such as Sweden and Germany) where vocational education has been seen as a high-quality preparation for worthwhile jobs – the more so as general diplomas in secondary and even higher education no longer provide such privileged routes into the labour market as they once did.

Countries that want to improve the status of vocational routes therefore need to ensure that employers perceive them as appropriate preparation for particular jobs – including those requiring high skill levels. One element of obvious importance is the relevance of specific skills being taught in a vocational field to current practice in the workplace (training centres described in case studies 7 and 8 address this aspect). Another, less obvious but of growing importance, is the way in which these specific vocational studies are combined with more general learning. In the modern world, an electrical engineer who leaves college with the necessary skills to write coherent reports for his colleagues, to understand the budgetary implications of a proposed new electrical installation, and to keep himself abreast of technology as it develops, has far greater prospects than one whose only skill is to design a new wiring system.

Thus, vocational education needs to maintain close links with employers and their technical requirements and at the same time see to the continuing intellectual development of its students. It has not always succeeded; indeed, in some countries (such as the United States) vocational schools have come under fire for allegedly doing neither job effectively. On the one hand, they channel pupils into educational ghettos reserved for less able pupils who have given up on "academic" studies; on the other, they are out of touch with the technical skills that employers want.

Partnership between vocational schools and employers is an obvious way of making studies more relevant to employer needs. But are partnerships able to foster a better balance between narrowly vocational and more general studies? In some situations, yes, as will be seen below. But the problem poses some fundamental dilemmas for vocational systems. These relate to the second of the issues referred to at the beginning of this section: the respective roles of employers and schools in delivering vocational education. There are, broadly, two competing models: "employer-led" systems, and "education-led" systems.

The main example of an *employer-led* system of vocational preparation in OECD countries is the "dual system", dominant in Germany, Austria and Switzerland. Apprentices recruited and paid by employers spend one or two days a week in vocational schools, and the remainder with the firm learning a trade. This system is widely recognised as producing high-quality vocational education and training, through a well-developed partnership involving not just individual employers and vocational schools but also the federal and state governments, trade unions and local chambers of commerce – who co-ordinate provision and run the final examinations.

The vocational schools (*Berufsschulen*) are quite clearly the "junior" partners in this arrangement. Apprentices spend most of their time in the company that pays their wages, that will eventually employ them and has the greatest say (along with other companies) over the curriculum. This dominance of employers has helped ensure that apprentices acquire the skills that they will need in their future careers.

But as technology and work become more complex, some people are starting to ask whether employer domination of the dual system could carry some potential weaknesses. Apprenticeships have proved an excellent means of passing on specific craft skills, but are employers able to cater for the broader body of knowledge and competences required in many occupations today? In fact, large German companies have responded to this challenge by broadening the scope of their programmes, and conducting a greater proportion of teaching in their own training centres rather than on the job. Small firms have found this difficult, but arrangements allowing them to group together to provide training centres have helped. There are nevertheless limits to off-the-job elements, whether in training centres or vocational schools, in a scheme paid for by individual employers. Companies will always require apprentices to engage in some form of productive work to help make their participation viable.

Another concern with the dual system, which is much harder to resolve, is the early break with general education made by its participants. Over half of German teenagers enter the system, at age 15 or 16. Few ever return to full-time education. It is valid to question whether that pattern will be desirable in the decades to come: not only will workers need a higher level of general intellectual ability than in the past, but they will need to continue learning throughout their working lives. (The more initial education one has, on average, the more likely one is to return to education and training as an adult.) In the 1990s, the final judges of the dual system will be its potential participants. Young people flocked to join it in the 1980s – including many who already had the academic *Abitur* exam – at a time when a large cohort of school-leavers coinciding with rising youth unemployment made apprenticeship an attractive route to a job. With a sharp fall in the size of the age cohort, the situation is changing. Demand for basic manufacturing apprenticeships has declined; young people are becoming more inclined to choose routes involving higher qualifications and good career development. To survive, the dual system may have to cater for those preferences.

Education-led methods of initial vocational preparation, which dominate in OECD countries, are the mirror-image of the dual system in terms of advantages and disadvantages. On the one hand, they can effectively combine vocational studies with relevant general studies, and in the process retain a high proportion of the population at school beyond the compulsory leaving age. On the other, schools may find it hard to keep in touch with the approaches and technologies being applied in real workplaces.

Perhaps the most successful example of this model has been in Scandinavia, where pupils aged 16-19 opt for either a general or a vocational upper secondary school. A pupil who wants to become a waiter, for example, will join a programme teaching every aspect of catering, and at the same time improve native and foreign language skills as part of a continuing general programme. Such broad "rounding-off" to the education of most citizens helps support the ethos of every worker being well-trained and educated.

Yet, even in Scandinavia, there are concerns that vocational schools are out of touch. An extra year has recently been introduced in Swedish vocational programmes to increase the amount of time spent gaining work experience with firms. New partnerships are helping to ensure also that students get access to up-to-date equipment, which schools could not afford to provide on their own. That does not only mean pupils visiting firms; *Huddingegymnasiet,* a school near Stockholm, has set up its own technical centre with machinery hired out to nearby companies as well as being at the disposal of its pupils.

In some countries, school-based vocational education suffers considerably from its low-status image. In France, for example, the *lycées d'enseignement professionnel,* which are now intended to offer an alternative route to the sought-after *baccalauréat,* are in practice chosen largely by students unable to get into other types of *lycée.* The quality of professional training on offer has been criticised, and there is a widespread fear that few pupils will use the new *bac professionnel* as a stepping-stone to further education and training. Some commentators now ask whether France might not be better off with a German-style apprenticeship system.

There are some signs of convergence between employer-based and school-based vocational systems – as the dual system becomes less focused on on-the-job learning, and vocational schools try to strengthen their links with the world of work. In the process, new relationships between employers and educators are being explored. Case studies 7 and 12 show two ways in which partnerships attempt to improve the French *lycées professionnels*– in one case by giving pupils and teachers contact with the most advanced technology, in the other by retraining teachers with the help of companies. Certainly the regular experience of work now built into the curriculum of French vocational pupils appears to have made teachers in these schools much more sensitive to the needs of companies.

A more fundamental approach, being tried in a few cases, is to attempt to re-position vocational and technical education within the school system. This is done in various ways in three fascinating examples in Italy (case study 9), Austria (study 10) and Germany (study 11). All attempt to upgrade vocational education within schools to allow it to be integrated with studies leading to the hitherto "academic" exam qualifying secondary school students for university. It would be unrealistic to suppose that such programmes could be extended to most students at present engaged in vocational studies. But they give a good idea of how the divide between vocational and "academic" education can start to be broken down. In the German example (case 11), it is not just the *Abitur* candidates but also apprentices who seem able to benefit from a more balanced mixture.

Will employers see the advantages of such a balance? Some are already active in trying to improve the general skills being taught in vocational schools – for example in efforts of a Virginia school in co-operation with nearby companies to improve its curriculum (case study 6). In the long term, employers want a workforce with a high-level, rounded education. In the short term, however, there is sometimes pressure to get recruits with specific skills, and to get them quickly. In times when school-leavers are relatively scarce, employers competing to recruit them may be tempted to forget the longer-term value of encouraging them to continue with higher-level studies. But much also depends on the state of the economy: a boom tends to cause more young people to be lured away from education into jobs; a recession the reverse.

Partnerships and the transition to work: the compact experiment

One of the greatest spurs to school-business links has been high youth unemployment. During the recession of the early 1980s, when youth unemployment rose faster than general unemployment, teachers and others started to worry whether large numbers of teenagers leaving school were being regarded as "unemployable". More recently, there has been a perception of "skills shortages" in the economy, coinciding with still considerable youth unemployment levels. The conclusion of many observers is that job opportunities could be made available for young people if only they came up to the standards required by potential employers.

Compacts are an attempt to bridge the gap between employers' basic expectations of their recruits and the characteristics of school-leavers. They are local coalitions based on the concept of a simple deal: jobs in exchange for basic, agreed standards achieved by school-leavers. In fact, this deal is generally only the first step in a relationship that tends to include a wide range of partnership activities. But the idea of exchange between education and business is an appealing one, which helps bring together a wide range of participants for a common purpose. The link with jobs, however arbitrary, also makes it possible to identify solid results in relation to the local economy. In other words, compacts are diverse partnership coalitions with a focus on recruitment.

The first, most famous, compact provided both an example and a lesson for future ones. Boston was an ideal city for such a project: flourishing city-centre business existed a stone's throw from some of the country's most severe educational deprivation. When in 1982 the city's warring factions – the schools, the city administration and the business community – came together to announce the compact, an enormous amount of goodwill and enthusiasm was released. Formally, the compact entailed an agreement by business to hire specified numbers of high-school graduates in the coming years, in exchange for the school department's pledge to reduce drop-out and absentee rates by 5 per cent a year and an enforcement of requirements on academic standards. Informally, the compact was about much more. "The most important thing is that it has opened lines of communication with the business community", commented the city's school superintendent[5]. Businesses, in short, became actively involved in school improvement programmes.

In the event, the formal pledges made in the Boston Compact were a mixed blessing. The business community certainly fulfilled its side of the bargain, offering from the start more jobs than had been pledged, and eventually more than the graduates involved could take up. The scheme also appeared to increase job equality: in 1985, slightly more graduates found jobs than in other U.S. cities, whereas the proportion of black graduates finding jobs was twice the national average. But the schools did not meet all their targets for improvement. Student performance rose sharply, attendance at a somewhat slower rate than pledged, but drop-out rates actually rose rather than fell.

That disappointment did not lead to immediate acrimony, but after the departure of the school superintendent and some other significant leaders in 1985, the spirit of the compact was changed. A new approach incorporating the compact into the school board's own improvement programme was launched by the new superintendent. The compact remains a significant alliance in Boston, lobbying for education spending and helping to find summer jobs for young people, amongst other things. But it only loosely resembles the initiative announced in 1982.

The compact is perhaps the one type of partnership that has been spread consciously across international borders. Boston has become a Mecca for Europeans wanting to start them up – but its pilgrims have been careful to translate the programme to suit local circumstances, and also to learn from Boston's experience. They have learned that the idea of a deal between schools and businesses linked to student performance and recruitment can help generate enthusiasm, but has to be handled with care. In both Hull and Rotterdam, two cases studied in this report (numbers 16 and 17), particular care has been taken not to make commitments that cannot be fulfilled. Confidence-building is seen as a long-term process, not as a sudden explosion of goodwill which might later be followed by disappointment.

For behind the compact model lie some tricky tensions. Why should employers promise to recruit school-leavers simply because they can demonstrate such basic achievements as punctuality and modest academic success? On the whole, these achievements are surrogates for something that employers feel is lacking in many young people: motivation. But in practice, developing motivation in potential drop-outs has proved a far more complex task than simply offering a "job guarantee". To help change secondary schooling to motivate children, businesses have to go further, getting involved, for example, in the kinds of activity described above in the section on general education. On the whole, businesses involved in compacts have realised this. But at the same time, the job guarantee element has been an important factor in launching the compact, and its functioning contributes to the project's perceived success. Thus, business involvement in a compact operates at two levels – making a deal with schools, and helping them to improve. The deal must be seen to work to continue stimulating wider co-operation; at the same time, such co-operation may be necessary to enable schools to fulfil their side of the deal.

Partnerships and the teacher: breaking the closed circle

Most partnerships that attempt to improve education are rightly aimed primarily at pupils. But few succeed without also influencing their teachers: businesses will never have a permanent presence in the classroom, and any thoroughgoing change must involve professional educators.

A partnership is an ideal opportunity to widen a teacher's horizons. A large proportion of teachers have spent their entire lives in educational institutions – first as pupils themselves, then as students of education, and finally teaching in a school. Yet most of their pupils will have to survive in a world outside education which the teachers have never known. The only way to avoid this problem entirely would be to stipulate that every teacher must have had a previous career – a rule of questionable desirability and total impracticability. A more realistic second-best solution is to ensure that teaching itself involves greater contact with the outside world.

The most obvious way of increasing teachers' understanding of the world of work is to enable them to spend some time there. Schemes to promote such contact have ranged from year-long secondments to one-day visits. Not all experiences are happy ones; teachers often have difficulty finding a role in a strange workplace, and are potentially less adaptable than their pupils. The schemes that have worked best, therefore, have been carefully planned, and usually related to follow-up work back in the classroom. A good example is described in case study 13.

What do teachers learn from contact with business? Most obviously, the types of skill that workers need. Many teachers are surprised to find out how important general thinking and communications skills are to employers, as opposed to specific vocational competences. But vocational teachers can also learn much about how processes in a particular industry are changing, and what that means for skill requirements. In some cases, it means revising the vocational curriculum, or changing the balance of teachers in various subjects. Case study 12 describes a scheme in which teachers in vocational schools were required to reassess entirely their contribution and its relevance to modern industry.

Teachers spending time in companies can also pick up useful ideas about their own working methods. In particular, the "problem-solving" style based around work teams which dominates in many work settings can be translated into the classroom. By observing company training activity, teachers can also get ideas about their teaching styles. As will be seen below, such lessons do not have to be one-way. But on the whole teachers have found it enlightening to observe how people learn in an environment completely different from a school.

Partnerships and the school: exploring new styles

If teachers need to avoid being monks, schools must not become monasteries. But schools have traditionally been run along very particular lines, making little active attempt to borrow methods such as management practices from other organisations. It is true that schools are not businesses: their objectives, their clientele and their responsibilities differ from those of other organisations. But while maintaining that difference, there is plenty of scope for lessons to be learned from other organisations. For example:

– *Managing budgets:* In most state-run systems, school budgets have been controlled by central or local government bureaucracies. Some school systems are now starting to adopt the philosophy of many large companies – that resources will be most efficiently deployed if budgetary control is devolved to managers at the operational level. Translated into education, that means head teachers running budgets. Many head teachers are ill-prepared to perform this role, and could well benefit from training in private-sector techniques.

In some cases, the devolution of budgets to schools is linked with the idea of partnership – in the Netherlands, for example, schools are being given greater independence specifically to increase their flexibility in dealing with business. Yet nowhere does there so far appear to have been a systematic attempt to pass on budget management skills from companies to schools: head teachers have not been flocking to business school on company scholarships. Perhaps they soon will. But in the United Kingdom, where devolved budgets have been accompanied by stronger business representation on the boards governing individual schools, business governors are already lending their own financial expertise in considerable numbers.

– *Managing people:* School teachers spend much of their working lives away from other adults. The prevailing management style in schools is to allow teachers to operate with considerable independence, guided by professional judgement rather than top-down orders. That has produced many positive results which might well be emulated in other walks of life. But there is a growing realisation that teachers also need to work as teams – not least because they are increasingly confronted with disadvantaged children whose problems have social aspects that demand co-ordination between the various adults with whom they have contact. Teachers seconded to firms witness an environment where adults are in one another's company all day long. That experience can produce new ideas for co-operation in schools. Similarly, schemes that bring outside adults into schools to organise cross-disciplinary projects may help break the ice between teachers who have hitherto regarded one another as competing professionals.

– *Managing objectives and managing change:* A head teacher typically spends much of the working day as a ''fire-fighter'' – responding to crises as they arise. Many heads, of course, steer ambitious programmes for change through their schools. But the approach that has become fashionable in private-sector management – of systematically identifying goals in order to define an organisational strategy – is not yet standard practice in education.

Partnerships have helped schools to ask themselves some fundamental questions about how they are run. The ''school restructuring'' movement in the United States is one example. Case studies 14 and 15 describe examples of schools that have questioned the structures of the past: the grouping of classes, the management of time, the location of teaching activities, and so on. In both cases, while change has been managed by educators, an essential input has been the stimulation of outsiders who first ask the question: ''why not do things differently?''.

A ''bottom line'' for business?

This chapter has so far dealt with the ways in which partnerships are helping to change education. But how does it affect the businesses involved, and what do they gain from it? An education system that better prepares young people for their working lives is of collective benefit to employers. But in most situations, no more than a small proportion of pupils involved in a particular scheme will go on to work at the company involved (apprenticeships are a significant exception). So the return to an individual company on its contribution to change in education is small. Many businesses are nevertheless willing to make such a contribution, either for altruistic reasons or as part of an understanding among the business community that a common effort will work to everyone's advantage. In making what is often referred to as a ''strategic investment'' in education, businesses hope that their employees will be better prepared not only for work but for future learning as adults.

Yet, specific benefits to individual firms can play an important role in partnerships. They may help justify a company's participation, particularly to boards of directors or shareholders. Equally importantly, they can strengthen the relationship between schools and businesses by transforming it from a one-way form of aid into a genuine partnership with gains on both sides, including changes to business behaviour in directions favoured by educators. Such benefits may be grouped into three categories: those that are direct

Table 3.2. **Recruitment and school links – Two examples**

Carpentry shop with 70-80 employees, with work experience programme and management keen to promote good student and school contact

• *Staff hiring through student and school contacts*	*Cost:* SKr (000)	• *Traditional staff hiring*	*Cost:* SKr (000)
Management's student and school contacts (160 hours)	48	Advertising costs	20
Work experience programme (lower secondary school) – including supervision, food and clothes	25	Telephone interviews: 70 applicants (12 hours)	3
		Interviews with 10 selected applicants (10 hours)	2
Administrative costs for work experience programme	7	Wage costs for five new employees – who failed on job and left	81
Result: more students apply to woodwork programme in upper secondary school. Of these, the company hires four per year.		Supervision for these five (736 hours x 20 % x SKr 110)	16
		Result: three employees stay on.	
Total: four recruits	80	Total: three recruits	122
On-the-job training: 25 % x annual wage cost	198	On-the-job training: 50 % x annual wage cost	297
Supervision costs	66	Supervision costs	50
Total hiring cost	344	Total hiring cost	469
Hiring cost per new employee	86	Hiring cost per new employee	156

Result: SKr 70 000 per new employee saved through good student contacts

Manufacturing company with approximately 700 employees, running work experience for lower secondary pupils and an experimental in-house vocational training programme at upper secondary school level

• *Staff hiring through student and school contacts*	*Cost:* SKr (000)	• *Traditional staff hiring*	*Cost:* SKr (000)
Work experience programme (lower secondary school) – including administration, supervision and clothes	50	Open house: advertisements, overtime compensation and refreshments	63
Result: more students apply to company's upper secondary training programme (for 10 students over 32 weeks)		*Result:* 50 applicants, with interviews	6
Planning (64 hours)	8		
Training of supervisors	32		
Reduced productivity: 10 % per supervisor	290		
Vocational studies teacher	123		
Student costs: food, personal safety equipment, clothing	75		
Government cost compensation for training supervisors	–5		
Government compensation of SKr 15 per student per hour	–192		
Result: all ten students hired		*Result:* 20 of the applicants are hired	
Total: 10 recruits	381	Total: 20 recruits	69
On-the-job training: six months at 25 % of wage cost	276	On-the-job training: six months at 50 % of annual wage cost	1 104
Supervision	0	Supervision: 15 % reduced productivity per student, for six months	1 296
Total hiring cost	657	Total hiring cost	2 469
Hiring cost per new employee	65.7	Hiring cost per new employee	123

Result: SKr 57 300 per new employee saved through good student contacts

Source: *Good School Contacts Pay Off,* brochure by Swedish Employers' Confereration (S-103 30, Stockholm, Sweden), 1991.

and tangible, those that are direct but intangible, and finally indirect contributions to the conduct and performance of the firm.

The most obvious direct gain to employers from involvement with schools is an improved recruitment potential. Young people coming towards the end of their studies may well be encouraged to apply for a job at a firm with which they have already had contact. Employers may get a ''free look'' at potential recruits by offering work experience. Even where recruitment is not the main motive for an employer's involvement, it can be a useful spin-off. That is particularly true at a time when the school-leaver population of many OECD countries is shrinking fast. As firms compete with one another for scarce youth labour, it could become increasingly important for them to establish links with young people before they leave school.

Can it be proved that direct contact with schools is more cost-effective than other methods of recruitment? One remarkable survey, whose results are summarised in table 3.2, shows that such comparisons are indeed possible. Several Swedish companies were asked to make detailed estimates of the cost of their school links and of recent recruitment exercises using conventional procedures. An important part of the equation was the extra training cost of recruits who had had no prior contact with their employers, and also their greater tendency to leave their jobs after a short time. In all firms, the final cost per recruit turned out to be lower using school links; the table gives two examples. The Swedish Employers' Confederation argues that all companies should try to make such calculations for themselves. It is using the figures as part of its campaign to strengthen links between business and all parts of education, including compulsory schooling. It tells companies wanting to promote a better understanding of their work that if they start with pupils as young as ten or twelve, they will reap long-term benefits.

Apart from recruitment, the most obvious potential direct benefit to companies from involvement with education is the productive use of pupils on work-experience placements. But in practice, this kind of benefit is rarely sought in genuine partnerships with schools: it is recognised that placements that are of real educational value are unlikely to bring an increase in production that significantly exceeds their cost. Trade unions are inclined to block any scheme where unpaid learners substitute for paid labour. Apprentices, it is true, may be regularly relied upon to perform certain routine tasks, but they are generally paid an allowance or wage.

The second category of benefit identified above is direct gain for the firm which is nevertheless too abstract to quantify. The most common example is public relations value. Few companies are shy about their involvement with schools, and most hope that it will improve their public image. Some of the companies most active in partnerships operate in industries to which the public has recently been hostile – such as the chemical industry.

As well as improving the image of an industry by proving that it is public-spirited, a partnership can also help brand recognition – not least among the pupils, who will soon become adult consumers. Most companies try to play down that benefit, which may cause concern among educators and parents. A company that manufactures cigarettes recently came under heavy criticism for giving a large grant to schools in Washington, D.C., even though it denied that its aim was publicity.

A further non-tangible benefit relates to the attitudes of employees. One reason for any company giving money to charities and other ''good causes'' is to make its workers feel good about the organisation. That is plain from almost any company newsletter.

Helping education may be a particularly effective means of increasing employee loyalty in a small community where workers in the firm have children at the school.

A third type of benefit, not often discussed but potentially important, arises from changes in a company's behaviour that are indirectly related to contact with schools. For example, a firm may adapt its recruitment and initial training programmes to reflect a better understanding of the education world and the potential of its graduates. In several European countries, schools are trying to move away from certification based largely on public exams, and offer a range of certificates such as "records of achievement". But many companies are nervous about recruiting on the basis of such certificates because they do not understand what they mean. Closer involvement in the education process can improve that understanding. Seen in this light, the problem of providing a smoother "transition from school to work" is as much about employers understanding what schools can provide as about schools understanding what employers require.

Can companies learn anything from teachers about pedagogy, in relation to the training of their own workers? Some managing directors hope that partnerships will contribute to the development of their own staff, but it can be hard to pin down such improvements in practice (see for example case study 13). Rather than having any noticeable impact on company training schemes, school-business links appear to supplement formal training by developing some of the personal qualities of employees. A worker doing a routine job in a factory may initially find it extremely intimidating to address a class of 30 teenagers. If successful, the experience may build the worker's confidence and make him or her more adventurous in confronting new situations and demands at work.

Thus, there are many ways in which firms can themselves gain from partnerships, but relatively few that can be measured in terms of their "bottom line" results. Some advocates of partnerships believe that working with schools, whose results are not expressed in terms of a financial bottom line, can itself be a benefit to company attitudes. Certainly few large corporations would today define their "missions" purely in relation to the profit motive. Schools are helping to develop the notion within business of the broader public good.

NOTES

1. "New Technology and Human Resource Development in the Automobile Industry", Paris: OECD/CERI (document for general distribution), 1986; "Changes in Work Patterns – A Synthesis of Five National Reports in the Service Sector", Paris: OECD/CERI (document for general distribution), 1989.

2. The skills referred to here are "generic" skills, or competences: the ability to work in teams, to delegate responsibility, to communicate effectively, and so on. They are distinct from skills related to specific jobs (e.g. the ability to lay bricks), and include some personal qualities and attitudes. Some generic skills, such as self-discipline and the ability to follow instructions, have always been important in the workplace. Where this report refers to "new skills", it means those that have recently become more important at work.

3. The Secretary's Commission on Achieving Necessary Skills, *What Work Requires of Schools,* Washington: U.S. Department of Labor, 1991. A similar list, covering skills actually required in the financial services sector, was drawn up by CERI in *Human Resources and Corporate Strategy: Technological Change in Banks and Insurance Companies,* Paris: OECD/CERI, 1988.

4. Colin Ball, ''Towards an 'Enterprising' Culture'', Paris: OECD/CERI (document for general distribution), 1989.

5. Eleanor Farrar, *The Boston Compact – A Teaching Case,* New Brunswick, New Jersey: Center for Policy Research in Education, Rutgers, 1988, p.14.

Chapter 4

PARTNERSHIPS IN CONTEXT: THE ART OF THE POSSIBLE

"By the year 2000... every school in America will ensure that all students learn to use their minds well, so they may be prepared for responsible citizenship, further learning, and productive employment in our modern economy." (National Goals for Education, U.S. Department of Education, July 1990)

The previous three chapters have identified many common elements among partnerships in different OECD countries. They have also suggested lessons that might be transferable from one partnership to another. It is always valuable to know what others are doing, if only to get ideas for one's own project. But at the same time, each project is shaped by its specific circumstances. Both the process of collaboration and the potential achievements of partnerships are constrained by context. This chapter looks successively at the importance of three factors: the country situation, the economic cycle, and the size of the companies and communities involved in partnerships.

The national context

Each of the partnerships studied for this report was strongly influenced by concerns particular to a national education system. Although many of the criticisms of education outlined in Chapter 1 are common to several OECD countries, reform movements have taken different directions related partly to the nature of existing educational structures, and partly to national culture. Even within a federal country like the United States, the language of educational reform in Kentucky has far more in common with that of California than with the United Kingdom or Sweden. These differences matter, because partnerships work best when they are going with the grain of educational reform, and may change little on their own. This section identifies some of the important "background factors" that cause partnerships to vary from one country to another.

The existing relationship between school and work

A broad distinction can be made between countries in which the transition from school to work is perceived to work smoothly under the present system, and those where there have been obvious frictions. Japan and Germany fall clearly into the first category; France, the United Kingdom and the United States are in the second, and Scandinavian countries fall somewhere in between. There has traditionally been a strong relationship between adult education and work, but problems have recently been identified with the initial transition from school.

The German dual system, described in the previous chapter, seems an ideal vehicle for guiding the transition between school and work – by combining the two in a coherent programme for those leaving full-time education. It is also the obvious vehicle for employers to influence education, and German partnership initiatives have focused on refinements of the dual system. In Japan, most pupils have little or no specific vocational preparation at school or university. But companies are generally happy to rely on their own well-established induction and training programmes for young recruits. That is partly because each firm likes to impart its own ethos to new employees, who may well stay until retirement. The process of moving from education to employment tends to be smoothed by large-scale advance recruitment of students in their final year of high school or university.

In contrast, in countries like France, the United Kingdom and the United States, previous methods of transition from school to work have broken down. These countries traditionally prepared only an élite minority to work with their minds; the majority who worked mainly with their hands passed straight from school into jobs with no systematic link between the two. Now that the intellectual requirements of most workers have risen, that system no longer works. So there have been efforts to produce better careers guidance, vocational education and work experience for pupils approaching the end of secondary school. But in addition, these countries have started to re-examine the suitability of the entire secondary education system in relation to pupils' futures at work. The conscious attempt to ensure that schools develop the competences needed in a 1990s workplace has therefore been stronger in, say, the United Kingdom than in, for example, Germany. So partnerships may have a more far-reaching impact on education in countries where traditional relationships between school and work have been weak.

The state of development of partnerships

The process described in Chapter 2, of partnerships developing more sophisticated strategies as they mature, applies as much to the collective experience within a country as to an individual project. In the United Kingdom and the United States, partnerships were initially aimed mainly at promoting contact between businesses and schools for its own sake; only latterly have they aimed to contribute to important changes in educational practice. Cross-fertilisation of ideas between schemes, and a progressive cultural change that makes business involvement in schools more socially acceptable, has made partnership a collective experience at the national level.

Collective perceptions have also helped develop the agenda for partnership in specific countries. Thus, in France the concept of *alternance* became popular in the early 1980s, and was a talking point for further reform in the early 1990s. Meanwhile, *jumelages,* or twinnings, between schools and businesses had also become fashionable. In the Netherlands, advocates of partnership most commonly hoist their flag on the cause of decentralisation. In the United States, the popularity of "adopt a school", which has often meant little more than financial sponsorship, may be giving way to the notion of "school restructuring".

Need the development of a collective wisdom about partnerships be confined to the national level? Certainly the education dialogue within nations has been far greater and noisier than communication internationally. The adaptation of the Boston Compact to different countries is the exception rather than the rule. Direct co-operation between partnership projects on an "exchange" basis (see for example case study 4) are promising, but still vastly outnumbered by intra-national contacts.

Nevertheless, there may be scope for countries to learn some broad lessons from the experience of partnerships internationally. The Conference Board of Canada, a national organisation that has vigorously promoted good practice in partnerships across its country, would like Canadian partnerships to learn something collectively from those in the United States – which have been commonplace for longer than in Canada. The Conference Board hopes that it can encourage people to skip the "feel-good" partnerships that for a long time dominated in the United States, and move quickly to coalitions that aim for genuine change in education systems. Judging from the impressive range of entries to the Conference Board's 1991 "National Awards for Excellence in Business-Education Partnerships", that strategy appears to be working. Certainly community-wide coalitions are a growing feature in Canada, as illustrated in case studies 20, 21 and 23.

This report, too, is intended to contribute to an international learning process. Its case studies, in particular, seek to illustrate what is possible. In countries where businesses have not moved much beyond providing work experience and training for young people, it takes a shift in attitude to see how they can become important actors within the classroom. Observation of how this transition has taken place in other countries may precipitate that shift.

Approaches to school and curriculum reform

Partnerships in the United States and the United Kingdom have much in common. Many are initiated by large corporations, but most attempt to involve individual schools in a variety of local links. Yet their outcomes are radically different. (For further information on this subject, see *Curriculum Reform – An Overview of Trends,* Paris: OECD/CERI, 1990.)

Virtually every partnership in British secondary schools attempts to relate to the themes of enterprise education and industrial understanding. These are promoted in the country's new national curriculum and its longer-standing Technical and Vocational Education Initiative, which has spread to nearly all schools. British partnerships are therefore part of a wider process of national curriculum reform. (It should be noted however that these and other comments related to the United Kingdom's new curriculum represent its aspirations rather than its achievements, but it is too early to appraise them. Some of its critics predict that, rather than strengthening earlier attempts to introduce an "enterprising curriculum", it will undermine them, by forcing schools to structure their teaching around conventionally-defined subjects).

In the United States, there are no such national programmes, with the result that partnerships pull in many different directions, sometimes but not always related to local school-board or state reforms. True, recent education secretaries and now President Bush have attempted to set a common agenda. This has produced some common themes, such as a stress on better science and mathematics teaching, and the inclusion of a stronger "core" of compulsory basic subjects. Furthermore, as illustrated in Figure 1.2, a third of partnerships now address matters of curriculum and instruction. But few school districts have attempted a thorough overhaul of the curriculum. (A notable exception, where a school-business partnership is co-operating closely with the district authorities, is described in case study 6.) One result is that many partnerships concentrate on matters peripheral to the school curriculum: structural change, assistance for disadvantaged pupils, and so on. One test of the national initiatives launched in 1990 and 1991 will be the degree to which they bring a greater coherence to the content of partnerships – in a way that has clearly happened in the United Kingdom since the Education Reform Act of 1988, which introduced a national curriculum.

Many Continental European countries are consciously attempting to link the national curriculum more closely to the needs of the national economy – although change is on the whole more gradual than in the United Kingdom, where everything was thrown open by the enactment of a central curriculum where none had previously existed. The trend in Europe is for progressive change to be supported but not led by partnerships: where projects attempt to go in a direction not yet approved by the national authorities, they are in danger of becoming not so much beacons as islands. Case study 9, for example, describes an Italian school working with local firms and others to develop new approaches to learning and work – which has had virtually no impact on the school system more widely, because the central government has not decided to generalise its approach.

The relationship between central authorities and schools

It is apparent from the comparison just made between curriculum reform in the United Kingdom and the United States that centralisation can provide valuable coherence in educational change, which in turn provides useful reference points for partnerships. Yet, individual partnerships work best at the local level, and over-centralisation can also be a disadvantage. Schools need to have the freedom to work with local businesses in their own way, and national curriculum criteria should not be so strict as to curtail all originality in the approaches of local projects.

In a number of European countries, partnerships will only thrive if certain central rules are relaxed. An exceptionally imaginative French project enabling lower secondary school children to learn in new ways by starting small companies has been diminished by rules forbidding children to handle money (see case study 4). In Italy, almost any experimental variation to the standard curriculum requires special legislation. In the Netherlands, a national commission recently recommended that the national government relax rules that deter schools from getting involved with local businesses (case study 24). Of countries with centrally-controlled school systems, Sweden has recently devolved power most thoroughly. A host of functions from the fixing of teachers' pay to the routine administration of schools have been moved from a national board down to municipal level. There are already signs that the new system will encourage a wave of new partnerships.

The United Kingdom is at present in an unusual and arguably favourable position, with a new element of centralisation that makes co-ordinated change possible, but not yet bound by inflexible rules. It has recently shifted from a system of substantial local government autonomy in educational matters to a firm role for central government in directing a national curriculum and related pupil assessment. The government has come under much criticism for the number of central powers that it has acquired. But this centralisation seems unlikely in the near future to hinder the types of partnership scheme described here, for several reasons. One is because curriculum guidelines are drawn up in fairly general terms. Another is because they embody many of the principles, such as "enterprise learning", that businesses favour. A third is because a tradition that has allowed teachers to innovate is unlikely to be lost overnight. And finally, the centralisation of curriculum has been accompanied by the decentralisation of management and budgetary responsibility to schools. (There is nevertheless considerable local scepticism of central government's role in British partnerships – related not so much to a fear of an overmighty State, but to the perception that schemes as delivered "on the ground" do not always match government rhetoric, particularly in terms of co-ordination between schemes and continuity over time. In short, the United Kingdom has developed a sophisticated model, but is sometimes accused of not adhering to its principles).

Cultural norms

Finally, the scope for partnerships in any country is influenced by the attitudes and norms of the prevailing culture. Americans' great appetite for experimentation has certainly contributed to the rich variety of partnerships that have been created in the United States. The dual system owes much to the sense of responsibility to community held by German companies, underpinned by the semi-official role of the Chambers of Commerce. Scandinavians' tradition of lifelong learning makes projects that bring a wide range of adults into contact with schools less of a novelty.

One aspect of national culture that is critical for partnerships is the relationship between business and the public sector. In most countries there has been some mutual suspicion between business and schools, which is now reducing. But that generalisation masks a range of attitudes. "Capitalism" has on the whole enjoyed a more respectable place in American society than in Europe. Even as attitudes change everywhere, that difference remains. In the early 1990s, Americans start to get alarmed when an entrepreneur – who has been making educational television programmes financed by advertisements for public schools across the country – suggests that he might start up a network of profit-making schools with commercial sponsorship. Even then, the leader of a big teacher union says the idea could have its merits. At the same time, many Europeans are still wondering whether it is healthy to allow business interests any part at all in influencing what goes on in schoolrooms.

The economic context

Both businesses and schools have been driven into partnership largely by economic considerations. In 1976, at the height of one of the worst economic crises in British history, Prime Minister James Callaghan made a seminal speech accusing education of failing to turn out workers with the skills needed by industry. The assertion of a link between economic failure and weaknesses in education has been a powerful stimulant for both schools and businesses to get involved in partnerships: schools for fear that their pupils will become unemployed; firms in the hope that a better-educated workforce will increase productivity.

If partnerships are stimulated by economic crisis, do they disappear when the crisis recedes? That question may be addressed at two levels: in terms of macro-economic or cyclical variations, and in terms of micro-economic, or structural change.

Partnerships that respond to rising youth unemployment tend to focus on the transition from school to work. Compacts, described in Chapter 3, are a good example: they attempt to revive the confidence of employers in school-leavers, at times and in places where few are being hired. Work-experience programmes may try to start to socialise final-year pupils into the working world, at a time when lack of experience might otherwise put them at the end of a long job queue. The severe recession that hit many countries in the first half of the 1980s encouraged such "Band-Aid" measures to mitigate the damage to school-leavers' prospects.

Macro-economic recovery in the second half of the 1980s did not mean an end to such partnerships, but a change in direction. Employers now wanted to hire young people – who for demographic reasons were becoming scarce – but often found that they lacked the necessary skills. Schools and businesses started to consider the structural changes that had taken place over the previous decade, and realised that the content of schooling may have to change. This shifted the emphasis away from the transition to work, and engaged partnerships in the content of schooling, both general and vocational. The mission of partnerships thus became longer-term, addressing problems in the economic and education systems that will not disappear overnight. Even as education begins to produce more of what employers need, the partnership mission will not be complete. Many partnerships are likely to become permanent features – like the German dual system – rather than simply measures to promote reform.

But in practice, macro-economic cycles could affect partnerships in another way. Companies whose business is booming, but whose profits are being limited by the lack of qualified labour, are inclined to devote generous resources to their involvement with education. In a recession, the long-term need to improve education does not disappear, but short-term means are reduced. When business is bad, companies are inclined to reduce spending on charities and on any item that does not contribute directly to bottom-line results.

It is hard to say, at the time of writing, whether the recession of the early 1990s is harming partnerships; even if it does not reduce their number, it might have curtailed their growth. But at the very least it appears to be encouraging companies to make partnerships more cost-effective. This may be no bad thing for education. Certainly large corporations that in the late 1980s boom gave large sums for the sake of making a contribution are having to think more carefully about how to make a real impact. They will also be considering what they get out of the arrangement, and are likely to pay greater attention to the range of benefits described in the final section of Chapter 3.

The context of scale

Much has been heard of the partnership initiatives taken by large corporations, that tend to be good at letting the world know of their achievements. Yet some of the most successful projects involve a school and a small local firm. A big company has the advantages of being able to duplicate a successful approach across a number of schools, and of being able to muster considerable resources for partnerships without making a significant impact on its overall budget. But a small or medium-sized company may be able to offer a school a more intimate form of contact with the world of work, in terms of both the content of the programme and the relationship between the partners.

An Italian pupil from the school in case study 9 went on two work-experience placements. One was in a small commercial bank, where he spent a week working with one of its employees using a software programme to devise a graphical analysis of cost schedules. His second placement consisted of a month in a large multinational manufacturing company, where he was rotated round a number of departments, and got a general view of how things worked. The pupil felt that he had got much more out of the first placement than of the second: by doing rather than observing, he had actually got a better idea of the organisation and how it worked. That would have been much harder to achieve in a large enterprise where a more general tour is necessary to understand how one process relates to another.

Small companies can also provide a favourable environment for pupils to appreciate some of the changing features of the working world. An increasing number of employees need to be concerned directly with customers, and with providing services rather than making things. This is true even within large firms whose final output is manufactured goods, but pupils are on the whole able to observe customer relationships and the nature of service provision more directly in small service firms. Small companies are also more likely to produce visible examples of entrepreneurship and risk-taking. It would be wrong to imply that small companies always offer superior work-experience placements: large firms are often better equipped to design well-considered programmes, and the functioning of large companies is an important aspect of the economy to understand. But the potential advantages of small firms must also be remembered.

A further difference is that schools may have a different type of relationship with a smaller company than with a larger one. A closely related question is the size of the community. In small towns in the Tyrol and in Yorkshire (cases 10 and 13 respectively), links between schools and a prominent local firm are greatly strengthened by community spirit, and the fact that many teachers, employees and pupils already know each other or are even related to each other. The sense of common purpose that is fundamental to partnerships is greatly increased.

Yet, for those who live in big cities, it is not impossible to imitate some of the advantages of the small community. The Learning Enrichment Foundation (case study 23) has managed to do so in a large urban district in metropolitan Toronto, by establishing a complex network of mutual assistance based around non-profit organisations, but involving people from all walks of life. Compacts, too, have succeeded in bringing together a variety of actors for a common purpose. The difficulty is that such co-operation is harder to sustain for a long period in a big city than in a small, stable community. It is hard to beat the links between a factory that dominates employment in a charming little Austrian town and the local high school established a generation ago by the firm's founder.

Chapter 5

CONCLUSION

"Education is too important to be left to the educators. The more people who are involved in changing it, the better." (Mac Prescott, President, Ottawa Carleton Learning Foundation)

In the past ten years, partnerships between business and schools have started to play a significant part in educational change. The extent of their role varies; in some countries, like the United States, business is now consulted as a matter of course in the preparation of most major education initiatives. In others, partnerships are still auxiliary, with the main decisions about education remaining with the State.

The 1990s will determine whether partnerships prove to be a passing fad, or whether they consolidate their position, to become a permanent, integral part of the education process. That will depend partly on the extent to which those involved in education, from ministers to teachers, accept the regular involvement of businesses and other employers in developing curriculum, teaching methods and other aspects of schooling.

A central conclusion of this report is that educators and politicians should indeed accept the integration of partnerships into the mainstream of their work. This is consistent with the priorities set by OECD Ministers of Education at their meeting in Paris in November 1990. The report has illustrated how business involvement can have a benign impact on education, rather than attempting to subvert its purposes. Of course, the nature of this involvement has to be adapted to local circumstances, and carefully monitored: as the sometimes sketchy results listed under the case study ''outcomes'' show, partnerships have not always been thorough in assessing their own impact; more detailed, independent evaluation is needed.

To consolidate their role, partnerships will thus also have to show that they are making a real contribution to education systems, going beyond superficial friendships between schools and companies. In the early years of co-operation, partnerships have been sustained by the novelty of contact and communication between two traditional adversaries. In this period of *glasnost,* it has not mattered much that initiatives have moved in a variety of directions without necessarily having a coherent impact on the system as a whole. Each project has seemed worthwhile in itself.

In the longer term, a form of *perestroïka* or system reform is necessary if partnerships are to survive the novelty of the initial contact. To sustain and expand their contribution to education, they will have to become viable long-term organisms – more than the pet projects of ''irrationally committed individuals''. Yet if they become institutionalised within the education system, they are in danger of betraying their initial purpose – to expose education to outside influences. This raises several issues for the future.

A balanced partnership?

In any long-term joint venture, it is important that neither side becomes unduly dominant. Yet, in partnerships between schools and business, a perfect balance of effort and initiative is rare. It is impossible to generalise, but a common pattern is that business takes the initiative early on, challenging education to become less isolated, but as a partnership matures and starts to focus on the detail of new learning strategies, business participants defer increasingly to the "experts" in education.

One way of countering this danger is simply for both sides to be aware of it. Partnerships start out with the idea that neither schools nor businesses have a monopoly of wisdom, and there is no harm in reiterating that message in the project's rhetoric. Another way of retaining a balance is to relate the partnership to issues wider than just the improvement of schools. This report has suggested that partnerships can also address the ways in which businesses' behaviour might change. That could help to make partnerships more symmetrical: if educators are attempting to suggest ways in which employers might behave differently, employers are likely to be less shy about bringing their own perspectives to bear on reform in education.

Challenger or collaborator?

A closely related issue concerns the stance of business as it gets more involved with schools. Compare the following two statements:

"Public education has put this country at a terrible competitive disadvantage...To be successful, the new agenda for school reform must be driven by competition and market discipline, unfamiliar ground for educators. Business will have to set the new agenda, and the objective should be clear from the outset: complete restructuring."[1]

"Working with education enables us to be better understood and, hopefully, respected by students and teachers and, through them, parents and the wider community. Such work enables us, as partners in the process, to support more effective preparation of young people for the rapidly changing world which lies ahead of them. Education, in turn, benefits from both curriculum enrichment and the greater public recognition of its importance, which involvement with the business community can bring."[2]

The first statement is from a company chairman, throwing down a stark challenge to the education world. The second states the philosophy of a firm with a well-established partnership scheme, emphasizing the collaborative nature of its involvement.

To work well, partnerships need both elements. On the one hand, this report has argued that partnerships are most effective when working in the same direction as other forces for education reform. Business does not have the educational know-how to dictate change to reluctant educators. It is most effective as a catalyst for changes that might otherwise move far too slowly. Yet, much of the benefit of partnerships will be lost if business participants seconded to work with schools end up with a perspective identical to that of teachers. One way to avoid that may be for big companies to consider carefully the emerging role of their "education-liaison" officers. These people play a crucial part both in facilitating link activities and in ensuring that senior executives and board members gain a better understanding of education and how it is changing. But the "liaison" professional should not be allowed to become a barrier rather than a link between teachers and employees. The danger is that those who are working permanently with schools lose the fresh perspective of the educational outsider. To retain that freshness, there needs to be a continuing input from employees at every level who are not involved full-time with education.

A broader partnership?

A further way of keeping new ideas flowing into education from outside is to broaden the scope of partnerships. For reasons discussed in Chapter 1, the most common new partners of schools during the 1980s were businesses. Yet, by opening their gates to outsiders, schools have also attracted participation from community groups, parents and others who consider themselves "stakeholders" in education. That trend can be expected to grow, for two reasons. First because there is a legitimate concern that schools should not be educating pupils purely for work, which represents but a part of their future lives. Second because many businesses are themselves trying to establish closer links with communities, and would like to use partnerships with schools as part of this strategy. Now that public education has become more than just a state enterprise, an increasing number of individuals and organisations will claim a stake in its future. With luck, the result will be a coalition of interests working together, not an unruly free-for-all.

NOTES

1. David T. Kearns, "Why Business Leaders Care About Education", in David T. Kearns and Denis P. Doyle, *Winning the Brain Race,* San Francisco: Institute for Contemporary Studies, 1989. Since writing this, Mr Kearns has been appointed Deputy Secretary of Education in the United States government.
2. *The BP School Link Scheme* (brochure), BP Educational Service, PO Box 30, Blacknest Road, Blacknest, Alton, Hampshire, GU34 4PX, G.B., 1991.

CASE STUDIES

The following 24 case studies describe examples of school-business partnerships in nine OECD countries. They are not intended as a representative sample of partnership types in these countries, nor in the OECD as a whole. Rather, their purpose is to *illustrate* some of the points made in the main body of this report, as well as to give some idea of the range of different schemes in existence. The cases have thus been selected to demonstrate a variety of features in a small number of examples. The fact that there are more examples in some countries than in others reflects only where interesting examples were most readily identifiable: no research has been done to compare the scale of activity in different countries.

To reflect the fact that these examples are not meant to represent national approaches, they have not been grouped by country. Rather, partnerships with common features have been put together. They have not been classified into specific types, since every partnership displays a unique combination of characteristics. However:

- cases 1 to 5 all relate to the general school curriculum;
- cases 6 to 11 relate to vocational programmes;
- cases 12 and 13 are directed particularly at teachers;
- cases 14 and 15 are based on school restructuring;
- cases 16 to 23 involve various forms of coalition.

Case 24 is an example of a partnership for change at the national policy level.

Most of the case studies were undertaken by the CERI Secretariat. Mrs. Anne Jones, an outside consultant, prepared case studies 18 and 19. The Canadian Conference Board assisted in the preparation of case studies 2, 8, 20 and 21. Mr. Eric Wallin of the University of Upsala helped prepare case study 22.

Further information about each of these partnerships may be obtained from the addresses listed in Annex 1.

LIST OF CASE STUDIES

1.	"DEC Challenge" – Enterprise simulation in Ayrshire	United Kingdom
2.	Distance Learning Project North – Technological innovation in Alberta	Canada
3.	Mini-Enterprise in Schools Project – A nationwide initiative	United Kingdom
4.	"Projet Lot" – Learning and enterprise	France
5.	Tioxide-Schools Enterprise Partnership – Learning "life skills" on Humberside	United Kingdom
6.	Chesterfield Technical Center – Curriculum restructuring in Virginia	United States
7.	"CERTA" – A technology resource centre near Paris	France
8.	"SOFIE" – An industrial training centre in Quebec	Canada
9.	"ITSOS Marie Curie" – A new style of school near Milan	Italy
10.	Reutte – An academic school and a metalworks	Austria
11.	Kollegschulen – "Hybrid" schools in Northrhine-Westphalia	Germany
12.	"Ariane" – Teacher retraining in Grenoble	France
13.	"Trading Places" – Teacher work experience in Yorkshire	United Kingdom
14.	Santa Fe School Improvement Program – Restructuring in New Mexico	United States
15.	Chiron Middle School – An innovative school in Minneapolis	United States
16.	Hull Compact – A city-wide job guarantee	United Kingdom
17.	Rotterdam Compact – A new route for at-risk pupils	Netherlands
18/19.	Compacts and TVEI in London and Birmingham – A tale of two coalitions	United Kingdom
20.	"Let's graduate Georgina" – High-school retention in Ontario	Canada
21.	Ottawa-Carleton Learning Foundation – A broad educational alliance	Canada
22.	Project Lindholmen – Plans for a "society of knowledge" in Gothenburg	Sweden
23.	The Learning Enrichment Foundation – Community development in Toronto	Canada
24.	The "Rauwenhoff Process" – A national policy initiative	Netherlands

CASE STUDY 1: UNITED KINGDOM

DEC CHALLENGE – Enterprise simulation in Ayrshire

"We want to change young people's attitudes to work at school." (Company official)

The partners

- Digital Equipment, Ayr. A computer manufacturer employing 1 500 people in a modern plant on a green field site.
- Pupils and teachers from five local schools participating in the Technical and Vocational Education Initiative (TVEI).
- The area's TVEI project team.

The project

A three-day enterprise simulation as an introduction to the 5th form (age 15+): 240 pupils split into ten companies, with teachers acting as "facilitators" and company employees as "consultants" to the pupils. The exercise involved buying materials, making a product and marketing it.

The main objectives

- To develop among pupils new attitudes to learning and work, incorporating the philosophy of the company. Specifically, the three days are designed to teach co-operation, dealing with change, and consensus.
- To strengthen the relationship between the company and schools, producing new perspectives for both pupils and employees.

Evolution

In 1988 the TVEI project team was looking for ways of enhancing local education-industry links; at the same time, Digital Equipment (DEC) was rethinking its education strategy. The company refused a request by the local education authority to donate equipment: it was more interested in influencing people and systems. But teachers on secondment to the company had had little idea of what they could achieve there. DEC Challenge emerged as one of several schemes trying to foster a better two-way understanding. The scheme is being progressively refined; for example a special software programme was designed to manage the third annual DEC Challenge in June 1991.

Outcomes

Both the company and the TVEI team are convinced that the scheme has changed pupils' attitudes to their fifth-year secondary studies. That effect is hard to quantify, but an external evaluation of the local TVEI project concluded that those participating are better at working in groups and communicating than their non-TVEI counterparts.

For the company, the benefits are less tangible. There is a feeling that employees who participate are likely to learn more about teamwork, about young people and about teaching. But these effects appear to be fairly random, and the gain to the company is difficult to pin down.

Comment

This is an example of a partnership created by the desire of a company to change its approach to education links, combining with new approaches from the education sector – in the form of the TVEI scheme. The partners shared many goals, and were able to focus on the crucial issue of influencing students' attitudes, and devise a short but intensive exercise for that purpose.

But the scheme was also influenced by the company's own agenda. DEC wanted its stated company philosophy to rub off on students, and devised course goals specifically for that purpose. It also wanted to feel that teachers and pupils might bring something positive to thinking within the company. A consultant working with the scheme points out that industry and education have different ways of doing things, and believes that these differences need to be valued within partnerships, rather than trying to make everyone think the same. But when it comes to the employees, teachers and pupils implementing such schemes, there is a strong tendency to think primarily in terms of education learning from industry. Certainly gains to pupils were in this case more visible than gains to workers.

CASE STUDY 2: CANADA

DISTANCE LEARNING PROJECT NORTH – Technological innovation in Alberta

"All education, including a future distance education system, should focus on the student and therefore on learning." (Project blueprint)

The partners

- Alberta Correspondence School, curriculum support branch.
- Digital Equipment of Canada, Ltd.
- Over 100 Alberta schools.
- Alberta Government Telephones.
- Computer-based training systems (now Campus America).
- Five other institutions and corporations.

The project

Implementing a technology-based distance education system into Alberta's small, remote schools. The system supplements rather than replaces teacher-led classes, but permits a richer curriculum to be introduced in schools that have hitherto suffered from their small size. Innovative methods include satellite telebroadcasting supplemented by localised teleconferencing, and two-way graphical interaction which allows teachers and students to use visual materials as they talk to each other.

Digital Equipment provides computers and applied software to assist in computer-managed learning in the physical and social sciences, accounting and mathematics. Computer-managed learning provides teachers with the support they need to customise students' study programmes to suit their individual needs.

The main objectives

- To enrich curriculum in remote schools, and to help these schools remain open.
- To develop new technology-based teaching methods.
- To increase retention rates and help students graduate from secondary school.

Evolution

Distance education in Alberta dates back 60 years, but the basic method of correspondence by mail had not changed by the late 1980s. This scheme was developed for introduction in 1988 by

Alberta Correspondence School's curriculum support branch. Starting with a Computer-Managed Learning programme designed to deliver high school mathematics courses, the project was soon expanded to include distance learning throughout the province. Planning is now underway to develop a more comprehensive delivery of courseware and learning systems, for application in both rural and urban contexts.

Outcomes

A wider range of courses are now available to over 7 000 remote students. The provincial government sees the scheme as a significant step towards improving educational standards in the province: student retention, academic achievement and graduation rates have risen. But despite identifying such positive results, the partners regret not having built in instruments for measuring precise outcomes from the inception of the project. As part of the project, a computer data base is now being developed to improve such evaluation.

Comment

This project was conceived to tackle a problem specific to areas like Alberta with far-flung populations. Its primary focus has been on overcoming the disadvantages of small schools where several year groups often have to share the same class and teacher. But the partnership has also succeeded in developing new techniques of student-centred learning which could also be of relevance in urban settings.

Educators have been helped considerably in developing these new learning tools by the expertise of their private sector partners in fields such as software design and networking. Conversely, a particular benefit for the computer companies is the chance to enrich their understanding of the educational process, and thus to enable them to develop more saleable products for this market. The logic of this partnership is therefore strongly rooted in a mutual interest: to develop technology for use in education.

CASE STUDY 3: UNITED KINGDOM

MINI-ENTERPRISE IN SCHOOLS PROJECT– A nationwide initiative

"I think this project has changed my approach to teaching." (School mini-enterprise organiser)

The partners

- National Westminster Bank – one of the country's "Big Four" banks.
- The Department of Trade and Industry.
- Most secondary and middle schools in England and Wales.
- Some local businesses; many adults other than teachers.

The project

A scheme to encourage schools to run small businesses or co-operatives, usually of short duration. Enterprises get a grant of £40 as start-up capital, and may apply for a loan of £50 from their local National Westminster Bank branch. A central Mini-Enterprise office at Warwick University together with regional co-ordinators give schools extensive advice and materials.

The main objectives

- According to the scheme brochure: "Education *for* enterprise" (how to set up a business), "Education *about* enterprise" (how industry and commerce work) and "Education *through* enterprise" (promoting team-work, initative, decision-making, etc.).
- The Department of Trade and Industry, which initiated the scheme, was concerned about the supply of budding entrepreneurs.
- Schools use the scheme to strengthen links in their communities, to improve the quality of project work and for a variety of other educational goals.
- National Westminster Bank shares many of these objectives, and in addition aims to improve understanding of banks, financial transactions and basic accounting principles.

Evolution

Set up in 1985, the scheme's original ideal was to get a mini-enterprise going in every school in the country – after two years it had achieved an impressive 60 per cent. In the initial stage, the stress was on spreading enthusiasm for mini-enterprises *per se*. Since 1987, there has been increasing emphasis on the teaching of "enterprise" more broadly, more so since "enterprise education'' has become a cross-cutting theme of the national curriculum introduced by the 1988 Education Act.

The shift of stress from the setting up of businesses to curriculum development culminated in 1990 in the scheme's merging with the Schools Curriculum-Industry Partnership – another nation-wide scheme. The merged organisation (encumbered with the acronym SCIP-MESP) is the country's largest body promoting the ''work-related curriculum''. This helps improve co-ordination between the various forms of enterprise education outlined above – and in particular to reduce the sometimes confusing number of schemes being offered at the local level.

Outcomes

A study on mini-enterprises carried out by Her Majesty's Inspectorate of Schools in 1988/89 concluded that they were generally well planned but inadequately followed up. The original goal of giving schoolchildren a taste of entrepreneurship has undoubtedly succeeded in terms of the sheer numbers of enterprises that have been created. The more ambitious goal of teaching them more enterprising approaches to learning has also been met in many well-documented cases, but patterns will vary greatly from one school to another. What is clear is that in the two years since the HMI report, there have been widespread efforts to bring enterprise learning into the mainstream of the curriculum – both through this project and more generally through the ubiquitous Technical and Vocational Education Initiative (TVEI). In this context, there is greatly increased scope for following up mini-enterprise projects in day-to-day classroom activity.

Comment

This is an example of an integrated approach to partnership at several levels: integration between enterprise activities and enterprising learning styles; integration between locally-generated initiative and nationally-centred guidance; integration of the goals of public policy with those of individual schools and companies. It would be misleading to paint a universally rosy picture, but schemes such as Mini-Enterprise and SCIP, along with TVEI, have helped create some co-ordination out of what a few years ago was a more haphazard set of partnerships in the United Kingdom. That demonstrates how a country's partnerships can mature with age – though in this case the process has been accelerated by the introduction of the new curriculum, and the central co-ordination that has necessarily gone with it.

Mini-enterprises have involved many adults other than teachers as individuals, but has the private sector as a whole had much input into their approach? The main private sponsor, National Westminster Bank, sees its most useful role as building its banking expertise into schemes where relevant; certainly it has not attempted to tell educators what the broader teaching goals should be. But like many industrialists participating in partnerships, NatWest officials involved with the scheme have become increasingly interested in broader educational matters, and now sit on various national committees. Thus, as the partnership matures, so do the objectives of its sponsors.

CASE STUDY 4: FRANCE

"PROJET LOT" – Learning and enterprise
"The pupils look forward into their futures." (School inspector)

The partners

- The National Education Ministry's office in the *département* of the Lot.
- Chamber of Commerce and Industry, Cahors.
- Banque Populaire.

The project

Work experience placements and mini-enterprises for 13 and 14 year-olds. The Chamber of Commerce pays for a liaison officer who identifies work-experience placements, which last a week and are available for children of every ability.

The mini-enterprises are each centred on a class, and simulate the establishment, operation and winding up of a real company over a school year. The start-up capital, of up to FF 5 000, is raised by issuing shares; the pupils involved prefer to keep control by buying a majority holding. While no pupil stands to gain or lose a large amount, this aspect adds realism to the simulation. The mini-enterprises get some advice from local companies, with the bank playing a special role *vis-à-vis* their finances.

The bank helps cover the project's costs and gives extensive help in kind; its total contribution is estimated to be worth FF 150 000 per year.

The mini-enterprises have been part of the European Community's "PETRA" programme, and have benefited from links with similar projects in other countries. Some ventures have become international, with market research and sales for products made in France being carried out in Ireland and Spain, and exchange visits being based on joint work on a mini-enterprise.

The main objectives

- To help break down barriers between local schools and enterprises.
- To allow all pupils to understand more about the world of work at a relatively early age, and thus to help them make decisions about their futures.
- To use enterprise as a learning tool.

Evolution

The scheme was the brainchild of Mr Guy Castel, a local inspector for the Education Ministry. When he approached the Chamber of Commerce with the idea, it had already been searching for a means of co-operating with schools, under pressure to do so from the heads of local companies. The partnership started in 1987; in 1990, the partnership between Ministry and Chamber of Commerce was joined by the bank.

While the work experience element has functioned smoothly, the mini-enterprises have encountered problems. The rules governing French schools forbid children to handle money in a commercial venture, so the simulated companies have had to rely on a cumbersome and unsatisfactory procedure to remain legal. In an effort to produce realistic simulations legally, the partners are asking the education authorities to change the rules for mini-enterprises conforming to a model set of procedures. In the meantime, the mini-enterprise activity has had to be scaled down.

Outcomes

Seventeen out of 20 of the *collèges* (lower-secondary schools) in the *département* and about 1 000 pupils annually participate in the work-experience programme. The number of mini-enterprises has varied, from a peak of 15, to five in the present period of reassessment.

Comment

There is a significant difference between the objectives and characteristics of a programme aimed at lower secondary school pupils and *alternance* or apprenticeships for older children. The aim is not to prepare them directly for jobs, but to transform their mentality. The scheme consciously labels itself "learning *and* enterprise" rather than "learning *for* enterprise" (the latter was a slogan of a former French education minister).

This idea is close to one now common in the United Kingdom – "learning *through* enterprise". One headmaster of a small school in the Lot has (exceptionally) made the mini-enterprise the central "learning tool" for his school. He has restructured teaching to allow several teachers of the same subject to regroup their pupils according to different learning situations rather than always having single-teacher classes with the same number of pupils. At the same time, the mini-enterprise as a common project for the school links into all disciplines – foreign languages through the exchange links, mathematics through the financial management of the company, and so on.

CASE STUDY 5: UNITED KINGDOM

TIOXIDE-SCHOOLS ENTERPRISE PARTNERSHIP – Learning "life skills" on
Humberside

> *"It's not just the non-academic pupils who need interpersonal skills."* (Company training
> manager)

The partners

- Tioxide – a chemical company, the world's second largest manufacturer of titanium dioxide
  pigments.
- Three secondary schools (Beverley Grammar, Immingham and Wintringham) on Humberside, where Tioxide has a factory.

The project

Each school was given £3 000 to spend over three years, to support an enterprise programme
which followed broad guidelines laid down by the company. Programmes were required to involve
young people in organising and managing, to relate to twelve core "life skills" identified by
Tioxide, link to academic as well as vocational subjects and produce lessons for other schools.
One-third of the money was controlled directly by pupils. As well as giving the money, the
company tried to transfer its training methods directly, for example by giving pupils a course in
group dynamics.

The main objectives

- To extend the teaching of life-skills from less able pupils to sixth-formers (aged 16-18) on
  academic "A-level" courses.
- To extend into education the training methods of a company.

Evolution

In 1986, Tioxide identified 12 "core skills" that were needed in schools. Labelled "the
GCSEs of life", they included the ability to make decisions, to resolve conflict, to negotiate, to
assess one's strengths and weaknesses. (GCSE is the exam taken by British pupils at 16.)

In 1987, the manager of the company's Grimsby factory invited schools to propose schemes to
develop these skills with 17 and 18 year-olds in "sixth form". The programme was implemented in

the three selected schools between 1987 and 1990. Their styles varied widely, from closely defined projects to a loose set of goals which students were allowed to develop.

Outcomes

All schools felt they had made progress towards developing the skills required. As an example of outcomes, Wintringham pupils formed a managing group which regulated projects ranging from a fashion show to a study of Grimsby redevelopment schemes. Pupils learned the importance of good planning (some schemes failed through lack of a well-developed business plan), learned more about interpersonal relations and how to deal with bureaucracy (for example getting round school rules in organising the fashion show).

The scheme has been followed up in a variety of ways. For example, Immingham has used it as part of an on-going programme for changing the style of its sixth form. An A-level studies enhancement programme uses "general studies" time to teach pupils new skills. The introduction of records of achievement for these pupils also helps to change the sixth-form ethos.

Comment

This project was a strong attempt by a company to extend its own training principles into schools. The view of the company trainers that their style and objectives can be transferred directly to sixth forms may cause resentment in some educational circles. The schools that took part came away feeling positive about Tioxide, believing that its approach had been most helpful. However, these schools had been self-selecting.

The distinctiveness of the project was its concentration on pupils studying for a traditional, highly academic exam. Its assumption was that these pupils will be just as much in need of "life skills" when they enter employment as the academically less able, to whom such courses have more usually been directed. There could potentially be a problem in taking time teaching these skills to a group of pupils whose qualifications will depend on their ability to pass written exams. However, it is encouraging to note that academic and life skills appeared in many instances to be complementary. Projects that build students' confidence and teach them to plan thoroughly have obvious spin-offs for academic performance.

CASE STUDY 6: UNITED STATES

CHESTERFIELD TECHNICAL CENTER – Curriculum restructuring in Virginia
"We want to sit down with classroom teachers and remould their thinking – with business people sitting right there with us." (School district superintendent)

The partners

- Chesterfield Technical Center: a vocational school for 11th and 12th graders in Chesterfield County near Richmond; enrolment 850. Its courses are taken by students based at the county's general high schools, including:
- Thomas Dale High School – enrolment 1 300.
- Philip Morris USA: a multinational manufacturing company, with a large factory in Chesterfield making mainly tobacco products.

The project

A scheme to develop a restructured curriculum based on the teaching of skills needed in industry. The reform will be planned and implemented by an Essential Skills Curriculum Task Force of educators, industrialists, parents and recent graduates, and by a co-ordinator. Though this project was only getting underway in 1991, it had a clearly mapped-out agenda, of identifying the needs, implementing change, and thorough evaluation. Philip Morris will contribute $125 000 a year for three years, to be spent on new equipment, extra teaching costs and other aspects of the programme. The Federal Department of Education is taking a close interest in the scheme.

The main objectives

- To remedy deficiencies in the traditional curriculum, especially with respect to the application of subject matter.
- To allow students on vocational tracks to continue at a high level of theoretical studies.
- To improve student achievement levels, and lower the drop-out rate.
- To enable employers to reduce their investment in remedial programmes.
- To produce a model that can be applied elsewhere.

Evolution

Philip Morris is a major employer in the area, with a workforce whose high age profile will necessitate large-scale recruitment from the mid-1990s. It is concerned that schools are not turning out students with the required skills, and has been urging the state to improve educational performance. In 1989/90 it organised a forum of local businesses, to persuade the state of the case for reform. Now there is considerable support for a more skills-oriented curriculum from some state officials, and also from the district superintendent in Chesterfield. That has prepared the ground for the present project.

Outcomes

The project has only just started, but the process of co-operation has already greatly improved understanding between education and industry in Chesterfield County.

Comment

If this project produces the desired results, it will have been helped by two major strengths. The first is a clear vision of educational change at the system level, which has been agreed in its essentials between the various partners, with support not just from the schools but from the education authorities. The district superintendent believes that staff development is the key to any change in the school system, and is prepared to devote resources to that area. For example, employers have been emphasizing the need to teach co-operative learning; so about three-quarters of teachers have been sent on courses in co-operative teaching techniques.

A second and related strength is clear-headed planning. The task force will not just be asked to make vague recommendations, but will set in motion a precise series of changes. On-going evaluation will be an important element, and will relate not just to school achievements but to experiences for the first five years in employment.

CASE STUDY 7: FRANCE

"CERTA" – A technology resource centre near Paris

"How can we intervene in this initial vocational training for young people to make them more effective?" (Scheme organiser)

The partners

- Renault, the car manufacturer.
- The national Ministry of Education.
- The regional authorities of Ile-de-France.

The project

A "resource centre for advanced technology" near Renault's headquarters in Billancourt. The centre models industrial processes with state-of-the-art technology, and offers week-long courses to schools in the region. It is attended by classes of students of industrial automation preparing for the *baccalauréat professionnel* or the more advanced *brevet de technicien supérieur*. They are accompanied by their teachers.

The model is designed to teach students how information can be transported around a factory site and used to co-ordinate a series of related processes to ensure uniform quality of product. Students take part in an exercise related to the making of a car part, ensuring that toolmaking, the measurement of part, the shaping of part, the washing of part and other functions are all brought into harmony.

The main objectives

- To give vocational students practical experience with advanced machinery, which is unavailable in their schools.
- To stimulate a better understanding of industrial processes, among teachers as well as students, and hence to provoke new methods of vocational teaching.
- To provide a resource for adult education, and a laboratory of advanced technology for Renault itself.

Evolution

The centre was conceived by Renault as part of its strategy to create a workforce that not only is educated but knows how to apply its knowledge. One element of this strategy is to give all new

68

Renault workers a general induction over their first three or four years of employment. A second strand, of which CERTA is a part, is to ensure that vocational training in schools is related to modern workforce practices.

The centre was conceived in 1985, and opened in September 1990. This long gestation period was due partly to the difficulty in negotiating a satisfactory agreement between the three partners, each of whom contributed one-third of the capital costs. It also took two years to prepare the highly complex technology of the centre, which continued to need refinement even after the opening.

The relationship between the partners was still evolving in the first year of operation. The education authorities proposed that the partnership, which had been set up as an independent organisation, be brought more into the public domain. Renault disagreed, and at the time of writing a solution was being negotiated.

Outcomes

CERTA is enthusiastically received by the students and teachers who visit it, as it allows them "hands-on" experience of technology, for which there is no substitute in a classroom. It is too early, however, to see results in terms of impact on teaching practices beyond the five days that classes spend at the centre. There appears to be some tendency in the centre's early days for teachers and pupils to regard the week as a one-off experience rather than as an integral part of their studies. The very sophistication of the technology sometimes appears to be the main object of attention, rather than the skills that it aims to teach.

Comment

This project demonstrates both how partnerships have enormous potential for breaking new ground and how their ability to achieve this potential can be limited by practical obstacles. CERTA demonstrates a method of learning directly through technology which could never have been produced in a purely educational setting. But will the five years and FF 34 million needed to get the centre started prove to have been well spent?

One problem is that the difficulties experienced in getting bureaucratic and financial agreement between the three partners make the regional and national authorities hesitate before repeating the experiment elsewhere – although Renault wants to do so. Behind this lies a more fundamental consideration in an education system that has been heavily dominated by a centralised State. There is a risk that projects initiated by the private sector generating insufficient enthusiasm from the public authorities are kept on the margins of education. Teachers may fail to integrate CERTA into their curriculum unless they get strong signals from the national education authorities to do so. It should however be emphasized that the project has only just begun, and these dangers may prove to be unfounded.

CASE STUDY 8: CANADA

"SOFIE" – An industrial training centre in Quebec

"...Custom-tailored training services using the latest technology... an increasingly coopera-tive approach which will focus even more on individual needs and self-teaching." (Scheme description)

The partners

- Area businesses.
- Davignon School Board.
- District of Bedford Protestant School Board.
- Government of Quebec.
- Government of Canada.

The project

The Townships Corporation for Industrial Training Inc. (SOFIE) is a specialised training centre set up by the region's school boards. The centre has the modern high-tech equipment needed to deliver up-to-date programmes, which is lacking in the region's existing vocational training courses. Courses cover operation and maintenance of industrial machinery, welding and machining; 85 per cent are delivered at the centre, and 15 per cent on site throughout the province.

The centre's management is overseen by a board of directors representing the partners. Government has provided the C$ 3.8 million initial finance required to establish SOFIE and purchase equipment. Business has provided further financial support, material resources and personnel. The school boards provide equipment and free use of space.

The main objectives

- To develop a skilled workforce.
- To facilitate learning among workers.

Evolution

The project was established in 1986, in response to the need for up-to-date training programmes. The region's school boards secured support from the Canadian and Quebec governments to establish the centre. Initially, the centre catered exclusively for workers and the unemployed, but from 1991, courses were also attended by students still at school.

SOFIE now plans to expand its activities to offer a wider variety of courses and services, and to sell its manuals and teaching tools to organisations throughout Quebec and beyond. Plans have been completed to bring students closer to the industrial environment by relocating SOFIE in an industrial park.

Outcomes

A substantial, sustained increase in the number of training hours offered to employees and others. In 1989/90, 1 790 people trained, including 200 non-workers. In 1991, it was estimated that 50 school students would be trained.

In 1990, the project began to monitor the experiences of students for the year after graduation. Results show that 90 per cent are employed, 85 per cent in fields related to their training. Quebec industries view the programme as cost-effective.

Comment

This centre was created to address the specific training needs of Quebec businesses and to provide workers and students with specialised skills. Although the need for the training was widely recognised, federal and provincial government seed money was required to get the co-operation underway. Once established, the centre's management and teachers were able to demonstrate to businesses and workers their ability to understand their needs. The centre consulted with companies on how to deliver effective programmes and achieve high training standards. Private support has remained strong enough to allow SOFIE to finance the building of a new site for itself, even though the government backing is coming to an end.

The partners believe that they have learned the important lesson that success depends on their goals being explicitly stated in writing, and that their respective goals, rights and responsibilities be documented.

CASE STUDY 9: ITALY

"ITSOS MARIE CURIE" – A new style of school near Milan

"My teaching has become more rigorous. Now I focus more on tackling specific problems or tasks." (Teacher, commenting on her involvement with work experience programme)

The partners

- ITSOS (Istituto Tecnico Statale ad Ordinamento Speciale) Marie Curie – an experimental school in Cernusco sul Naviglio, near Milan.
- The Italian Ministry of Education; its research institute (IRSAE); its provincial office.
- The Labour Ministry's research institute (ISFOL).
- Local enterprises, the Chamber of Commerce, the Association of (manufacturing) Enterprises and other community interests.

The project

An innovative upper secondary school developing new approaches to learning and work. Seen by the national authorities as a pilot for wider change in upper secondary schooling. Links with local companies focus mainly on the development of work-experience placements. The school has 1 300 pupils aged 14 to 19.

The main objectives

- To devise a programme which better orients pupils to the culture of work and to the choices available to them. To give every pupil substantial experience of work.
- To allow education to learn from the outside world, in particular by encouraging teachers to visit workplaces and consider how their methods of work, technologies and social environment might be applied in schools.
- To experiment with various new curricula.

Evolution

The school was founded in 1971 with just 70 pupils, and has gradually grown. In 1979/80, responding to a request by ISFOL to study the feasibility of *alternance* in upper secondary schools, the Catholic University of Milan worked with ITSOS to establish a new kind of work-experience programme (see "Outcomes"). In 1988, the school established a new course on entrepreneurship.

Outcomes

- A *"biennio"* (2-year cycle for 14-16 year-olds) that attempts to familiarise pupils with the culture of work, identify their own strengths with respect to the working world and enable them to make informed choices for their more specialised studies. In other Italian schools, careers guidance at this age is perceived to be lacking.
- A *"triennio"* (3-year cycle for 16-19 year-olds) that makes all students continue with a broad programme of general studies – maintaining a balance between science, social studies and the arts. Each student also specialises in a particular line, ranging from classical studies to electronics. In taking a specially-adapted form of the *maturità* (the school-leaving exam), pupils are encouraged to relate their special subject to other disciplines.
- A work-experience programme taken voluntarily by over 90 per cent of fourth-year pupils (aged 18) after the end of the normal school year in June. The placements last a month and involve concentrated hands-on experience of work. They are followed up by an assessment of the pupils' performance and of the appropriateness of school-based curricula in relation to the workplace.
- A course on entrepreneurship for selected final-year pupils. The school identifies those most likely to acquire entrepreneurial skills. The end product of the course is a substantial business plan created by a team of pupils, in a form that could qualify it for regional grants if turned into a real business after the pupils finish school.

Comment

ITSOS Marie Curie is labelled a pilot school, but its programmes have not been used as a general model for change in Italy, even though they have been imitated at some other pioneering institutions. This case is strongly influenced by the context of a highly-centralised national education system: special rules have been drawn up to allow it to experiment, but the degree to which the model is spread is largely in the hands of the Ministry of Education. This "all-or-nothing" context for change contrasts strongly with the situation in decentralised countries like the United States, where there is more scope for partnerships to play a role in *ad hoc* reform.

Nevertheless, this school's approach is of considerable interest in the international context. In particular, the immersion of all pupils in a month's work experience – including those headed for academic studies at university – is unusual. There appears to be a pay-off in terms both of how teachers teach and how pupils learn: both say they have become more focused, or task-oriented as a result. In addition, there is a conscious effort by the school to adapt its curriculum continuously as a result of feedback from companies. In this partnership, most of the initiative comes from the education side, but the educators involved are always ready to learn from industry.

CASE STUDY 10: AUSTRIA

REUTTE – An academic school and a metalworks

"We are dependent on the factory, just as they are dependent on us." (Headmaster)

The partners

- Bundesrealgymnasium, Reutte. A school of 540 pupils aged 11-19 in a small town in the Tyrol.
- Metallwerk Plansee, Reutte. A nearby metal factory with 2 000 employees, specialising in high-perfomance refractory metals and their products.

The project

A special programme for some of the *Gymnasium*'s 14-19 year-olds, which combines ordinary academic studies leading to the university-qualifying *Matura* exam with the study of metals and metalwork.

The programme links the school closely with the local metalworks, in several ways:

- All metalwork studies are taught in the school by staff from the factory, working extra hours for which they are paid by the Ministry of Education.
- All equipment, supplies and maintenance connected with the metalwork programme is paid for by the company, at a substantial cost: around $50 000 per year.
- Though most study takes place at school, pupils have a chance to observe the factory regularly, in particular where expensive up-to-date equipment is not available at the school.

The main objectives

For the company:

- To cultivate a future supply of senior employees with a combination of advanced technical with high-level thinking and language skills.
- More generally, to apply the philosophy of the firm's founder (that technical and intellectual skills should be complementary rather than mutually exclusive).
- Originally, to get a *Gymnasium* in Reutte – previously there had been none.

For the school:

- To offer pupils the chance of achieving high academic standards combined with a practical experience of industry and technical knowledge.
- To make use of the facilities, resources and expertise of a nearby company.

Evolution

In 1952, the school was set up as a private institution at the initiative of Paul Schwarzkopf, a prominent industrialist who had founded the metalworks in Reutte in 1921 and was now willing to pay most of the cost of having a good school in the town. The school's metalwork programme was set up in 1959/60; in 1968 the school became public; by 1975 the metalwork programme had been fully integrated into the public system.

Outcomes

Some thirty pupils who have passed through the programme – including Paul Schwarzkopf's own grandson, who will soon take over the family business – are now working at the firm. While this is small in relation to the total workforce, they are concentrated in marketing and R&D – two key areas in a business selling high-tech products around the world.

Some 70-80 per cent of the programme's graduates go on to university – about the same proportion as other pupils in the *Gymnasium*. Many end up working abroad, where they benefit from their combined strength in language and technical skills.

However, roughly half who start the course find it too difficult to complete. Typically these "drop-outs" go into apprenticeships, often at the metalworks, where they reportedly fare well even with this partial preparation.

Comment

This is an exemplary intiative producing people with technical know-how combined with communication and thinking skills. Its pupils feel that they have to work harder than their peers doing purely academic studies, as the metalwork element is entirely *additional* to these (though to compensate, the course takes an extra year). This feature makes the programme unlike technical or vocational schools in Austria and elsewhere, where the amount of general study is reduced.

The partnership gains enormously from the cohesiveness of a small community. The big financial contribution is underpinned by the commitment of a family firm, whose own children benefit. Pupils at the school gain further experience by working at the factory in their summer holidays.

The one big limitation of this scheme is its scale. Only about one-fifth of the *Gymnasium*'s pupils take part, and the model has not been duplicated elsewhere in Austria. So each year only about 10-15 pupils are benefiting.

CASE STUDY 11: GERMANY

KOLLEGSCHULEN – "Hybrid" schools in Northrhine-Westphalia
"Learning in this school is not compartmentalised." (Teacher)

The partners

- The 32 schools.
- The state (*Land*) Ministry of Education.
- Local firms under the apprenticeship system.

The project

A new kind of upper secondary school initiated in the late 1970s. Thirty-two schools are now open. They cater both for part-time students on apprenticeships under the German "dual system" and for full-time students studying for the university-qualifying *Abitur* exam. Students mix academic with practical studies to a greater degree than most German students. Apprentices get 33 per cent more school lessons than apprentices in ordinary vocational schools, in a wider range of subjects; in addition to the normal Chamber of Commerce vocational qualification, they may take general education exams – most commonly to qualify them for a *Fachhochschule* (polytechnic). *Abitur* candidates may also gain a "double qualification", by taking a vocational exam set by the state government, reflecting a strong vocational element in their work. Each school offers one or more "curriculum careers" – vocational fields which provide the focus for most lessons; there is a strong interdisciplinary ethos, with a stress on links between vocational and general subjects. The teaching style puts relatively high emphasis on students learning in co-operative groups rather than simply listening to a lecturing teacher.

The main objectives

- To achieve better integration between vocational and general studies.
- To give pupils a rounded view of a vocational field. To offer them the flexibility to make appropriate choices about career and further education paths, underpinned by a double qualification (vocational and general). At the same time to establish "group corridors" as routes to a profession, rather than offering each individual his or her own personal route.
- To break down barriers between subject disciplines.
- "To show the *Gymnasium* [academic high school] that there is more in life than Latin and classical texts...to show normal vocational schools that they must overcome the gap between vocational and general education" (school inspector).

Evolution

The *Kollegschulen* were founded as a result of a re-examination of the vocational education system in the mid-1970s, which involved both public and private sector actors. Although there was debate at the federal as well as the state level, most of the system survived without structural change: *Kollegschulen* were a notable exception. The first was established in 1977.

The schools have come up against considerable opposition from defenders of the existing system. Chambers of Commerce, who run the dual system, have been opposed, although many individual firms have been happy to send their apprentices to the schools. The *Kultusministers-konferenz* (KMK) – the collection of state ministers of education, which oversees standards – has been sceptical of the ability to achieve the necessary standard in the *Abitur* while studying for a vocational qualification as well. In 1988 the KMK ruled that *Kollegschule* students must therefore study for an extra year to get doubly qualified.

Outcomes

About 75 per cent of the full-time students enrolled for the *Abitur* plus vocational qualification succeed in getting them both. Of part-time students, most attempt only the Chamber of Commerce exam, but on average 15 per cent of students entitled to enrol for a double qualification also qualify for the *Fachhochschule*. Performance varies, as does the standard of student intake, according to the discipline: a school specialising in electronics gets as many as 70 per cent of its apprentices through the *Fachhochschule* entrance exam.

It is hard to identify precisely the impact on other schools. In the view of the state's inspectors, there has been little impact on the attitudes of the *Gymnasiums,* but more on employers and schools in the dual system. Although few employers have openly expressed a strong preference for *Kollegschulen,* some appear to be putting pressure on ordinary vocational schools to adopt some of the *Kollegschule*'s style (such as more group-oriented teaching).

Comment

The German dual system is probably the most mature form of education-business partnership in OECD countries. Its maturity gives it great strengths, but one potential weakness is that its institutions may be too entrenched to contemplate change where appropriate. *Kollegschulen* attempt to introduce a variant with new approaches in the schooling of apprentices. Their supporters claim that *Kollegschulen* are not intended to challenge the dual system, simply to offer a variant. But they have encountered considerable opposition, both explicit and tacit. For the time being they remain a small exception to a relatively homogeneous system.

CASE STUDY 12: FRANCE

"ARIANE" – Teacher retraining in Grenoble
"Ariane perhaps marks the end of adolescence for teachers." (Former scheme co-ordinator)

The partners

- The Grenoble office of the national Ministry of Education.
- Vocational high schools in the region.
- Local companies.
- University of Grenoble.

The project

A programme designed to "adapt, convert and place in new jobs" mid-career teachers of technical subjects with outdated skills. Teachers are released to take a programme of courses designed around their own needs. The courses may last from one to three years and involve elements of teacher training, general study at the university and experience within enterprises. Some teachers update their skills within their own discipline; others transfer to a subject in greater demand.

The main objectives

- To retrain in vocational subjects teachers whose skills relate poorly to new work requirements – either because workers in that field require higher-level general skills (e.g. mathematical ability) or because there is reduced demand for a professional category (e.g. textile workers).
- To give teachers some experience of industrial practices.
- To help companies and schools learn from each other when retraining workers.

Evolution

The scheme was a response by the education authorities to the mismatch between teacher skills and pupil demand at vocational schools. Some teachers, who enjoy job security as civil servants, were teaching classes with only one or two pupils. Ariane was largely inspired by the retraining scheme of a local company, Merlin-Gérin, which decided that all workers with outdated skills should be redeployed rather than being made redundant. The company worked closely with the project: some teachers were able to train alongside its workers; others helped with the training.

Ariane started in 1988/89 with 80 teachers; in 1990/91 there were 230. The initial model was to spend a year on general courses and induction, and then decide a training plan. With experience, the induction was reduced to a few weeks, allowing each teacher to take courses designed to meet individual goals.

Outcomes

A minority of the teachers (30 in 1990/91) succeeded in converting to new disciplines, although this represents 80 per cent of those who aimed to convert. A typical conversion was from teaching mechanics to teaching mathematics. The difficulty in making such a conversion (for teachers with relatively low levels of initial education) under strict inspection of the standard achieved helps account for the small take-up.

Most of the teachers thus opted to "adapt" their skills within their own subject area. There was no measurable success rate for this process: the idea, say the organisers, is to "create a dynamic" of self-training which continues beyond the end of the course.

Comment

"Certainly", says an astute French commentary on this project, "the delay in adapting to technological change forces [the education authorities] to act in haste; on the other hand, it allows them to draw on the experience of companies in redeploying workers." ("Ecole et Entreprises", *Revue Autrement,* January 1991, Paris, p. 41.) Ariane was initiated and run by the national education authorities, but attempted to draw on the wisdom of industry in two separate ways. First, by sending teachers into companies to find out what sorts of skills their pupils needed to learn. Second, by learning from industrial restructuring in the 1980s how middle-aged workers with outdated skills might still be retrained.

Increased contact has also made companies realise that they can learn useful things from teachers. Vocational high schools have always sent pupils out for periods of work experience; but the "tutors" they are assigned to in the firms are not always well prepared to help them learn. A feeling common to many French companies, that they could improve their own training by drawing on the expertise of public education, was reinforced by the project.

CASE STUDY 13: UNITED KINGDOM

"TRADING PLACES" – Teacher work experience in Yorkshire

"I am grateful for the chance to consider factory processes as analogous to school learning processes... Indeed any learning processes." (Teacher)

"I can't believe how much schools have changed. More human. More informal." (Employee)

The partners

- Prospect Foods Ltd., a small, family-run firm based in Harrogate, Yorkshire comprising a quality bakery, a tea and coffee factory and Betty's Cafe Tea-rooms – a well-known local chain.
- Teachers in 18 schools throughout North Yorkshire.
- North Yorkshire Schools and Industry Association – which worked with the company to organise the project.
- The Training Agency and the Hotel and Catering Industry Training Board – which helped fund the project.

The project

A one-year scheme offering teachers the chance of a short (3-day) placement at Prospect Foods, followed by a reciprocal visit of staff to the school. These placements were the starting point for many further contacts and school-based projects. A total of 27 teachers and 27 Prospect Foods staff traded places.

The main objectives

- To broaden the horizons of both teachers and Prospect Foods employees. The company's managing director was keen to develop his own staff, especially younger workers, as well as to provide teachers with opportunities to learn about his company.
- To build mutual confidence within local communities.
- To develop innovative cross-curricular projects in schools.
- To improve the quality of Prospect Foods recruits.

Evolution

The project took place largely at the initiative of Prospect Foods, a company keen on staff development and on links between adult learning and school learning. The company resisted

80

bringing other firms into the partnership but hoped that it could produce a model useful to others. The scheme took place in school year 1989/90, but has been followed up by numerous continuing contacts between Prospect Foods and schools.

Outcomes

Teachers and company staff are generally enthusiastic about having had the chance to see how another organisation works, even though quite a few initially had problems adapting to a strange environment. An indicator of the project's success is the considerable number of links that have continued beyond its formal life.

Many of the teachers had very clear objectives: they wanted to use the project as a tool for their own classroom work. One teacher, for example, used it as a means of getting the company staff to help run an "industry week". That teacher felt that simply inviting the company to send a representative would have been far less satisfactory; one aspect of "Trading Places" was that it involved young and relatively junior employees – with whom school pupils could more easily relate than with senior managers. Another teacher organised a multidisciplinary project in which 11 year-olds learned to make chocolates. The children sent the chocolates, with a letter in French, to pupils in an "exchange" school in France.

Benefits for employees were less direct, but the managing director is convinced that the exercise has contributed to their continuing education. In one instance, a young worker about to take on new responsibilities was able to gain markedly in self-confidence from his work in a school. More often, the benefit of operating in a new environment was more general, and the staff were not on the whole aware that this was the intention.

Comment

The success of this scheme for schools rested largely on two factors. First, good advanced planning maximised the classroom impact of a short exchange: one organiser reckoned that a teacher with a clear purpose could get more out of 3-day work placement than a teacher who spends three weeks in a company just "to see what it's like". Second, as with other British partnerships, a background of rich curriculum development gave teachers the chance to apply their experience beyond the confines of the project.

For the company, the success owed much to its commitment to lifelong learning for its own workforce and to involvement in its local community. The benefits of the latter are obvious in a small town like Harrogate: one teacher placed at the bakery found herself "work-shadowing" a former pupil, and then working next to the mother of one of her present pupils. In such circumstances, the notion of "lifelong learning" becomes more poignant.

CASE STUDY 14: UNITED STATES

SANTA FE SCHOOL IMPROVEMENT PROGRAM – Restructuring in New Mexico
"What if we did it another way?" (Project brochure)

The partners

- The Panasonic Foundation (an educational foundation set up by the Matsushita Electric Corporation of America).
- Santa Fe (New Mexico) school district.
- Santa Fe schools.

The project

An initiative to encourage schools to restructure themselves in various ways, each appropriate to their own situation. Panasonic stimulates such efforts by paying for visits from "consultants" with experience of reform in other school districts, and for Santa Fe teachers to observe progress elsewhere. The Foundation runs similar projects in seven other U.S. cities. In each case it makes a commitment to work with the area's schools for 5-10 years.

The main objectives

- To bring outside ideas for change into urban schools.
- To focus change on individual schools, at the same time as involving whole districts in reform.
- To challenge such conventional school practices as 50-minute class periods, fragmented curricula, self-contained classrooms and segregation of children by age.

Evolution

The programme was initiated in 1987. It had enthusiastic backing from the district superintendent, though many teachers were initially extremely wary. Panasonic's strategy has been to involve groups of teachers from each school in deciding what kinds of change are appropriate. Thus the scheme has gradually won the confidence of more (though not all) teachers, and all schools have now implemented some changes. The sudden death of the superintendent in 1990 was a serious setback, but the commitment of his successor has allowed the momentum built up over the previous three years to be sustained.

Outcomes

Restructuring has varied greatly from one school to another. At its most ambitious, the programme has helped a junior high school to convert to a "middle school" with more integration between learning in different subjects, and the division of the school into four "families" of pupils, which allows all the teachers of any one pupil to work together. Even in this case, however, short single-subject, single-teacher lessons remain the norm. Initiatives at other schools include: the combination of the first three grades (ages 6 to 9) into one; the setting up of "co-operative learning" classrooms; a textbook written by teachers; a summer tutoring programme; an early intervention programme for children at risk.

Comment

This is a partnership which stimulates change from within education rather than involving any great increase in local contact with business or other outsiders. But Panasonic's intervention is clearly essential to the changes taking place. All teachers involved acknowledge that if the Foundation had not raised the issue of restructuring and financially supported the exchange of knowledge and expertise, none of the changes would have taken place. Thus, the "business" partner in this case serves the role of the outsider challenging the system to change itself.

The reforms that result might best be described as minor systemic change: they involve new ways of doing things, but not the genuine overhaul of school structures or methods that some people are calling for. The strength of progressive change from within education is that it is more likely to be sustained than some more dramatic, fashionable innovations prompted by outsiders. The potential danger is that those within education will never sufficiently challenge their own approach to teaching.

CASE STUDY 15: UNITED STATES

CHIRON MIDDLE SCHOOL – An innovative school in Minneapolis
"A new community-based approach to learning." (Sign over school gates)

The partners

- A self-selecting group including business people, parents, educators, school board officials and the president of the local teachers' union.

The project

A new school for 5th-8th graders (ages 10 to 14) in central Minneapolis, with 180 pupils in 1990/91. Set up by a diverse group of people dissatisfied with the existing system, it is nevertheless a public school funded (except for some start-up costs) at exactly the same level as other public schools in the district.

Within those constraints, Chiron aims to develop new classroom structures and teaching strategies. Its most significant innovation is to hold classes at a range of sites other than a conventional school building. Its teaching style is "hands-on", informal and related wherever possible to real-world exercises.

The main objectives

- To create a school environment that motivates children to learn, allows them to understand the applications of what they learn, and teaches them how to think.
- To take advantage of "the rich educational resources of the community".
- To develop individual "family learning plans" in collaboration between teachers, parents and students.
- To devolve budget responsibility to a representative management council and curriculum development to the school level.
- To create a model that can be reproduced elsewhere.

Evolution

Chiron was conceived in late 1987 at the time of a controversial school-board election, when a group of Minneapolis business people, parents and others decided to look directly for better ways of running a school. After a nation-wide competition for ideas, the school was designed and opened by September 1988 – a gestation period of less than a year.

In the school's first year, students rotated every twelve weeks between its three community-oriented sites. At a college in downtown Minneapolis, the emphasis was on economic and government activity. On a university campus site, the children had contact with scientists and were able to observe natural phenomena first-hand in their science studies. In a building near various theatres and galleries, teaching focused on the arts.

But the organisation of that system put too much strain on staff resources, and in the second year the programme was reluctantly modified, with a more or less conventional school building acting as a base, though with frequent site visits built into the curriculum. A further modification being envisaged is a greater ratio of pupils to staff: the relatively low number of 20 children to a class will be hard to sustain if teachers are allowed time for professional development. The attempt to construct imaginative programmes with no extra resources has already placed unacceptable stresses on staff time, and only two out of the six original teachers remained after the first year.

Outcomes

Chiron's teachers most frequently measure their success in terms of enthusiasm of the pupils: most of them cannot wait to get to school and learn, despite the fact that many had difficulties at previous schools. Performance on the school district's "benchmark" tests is average, but Chiron also wants to develop broader measures of student achievement.

Comment

Chiron was born of a genuine coalition of community interests, and has produced promising new approaches to learning. It is unusual in its attempt to depart so radically from conventional school structures while still remaining within the public school system and serving the ordinary child.

Why did this school have to modify its aims so drastically within a year of opening? Clearly the breakneck speed with which the idea was implemented created some problems – but this is not the whole answer. The biggest single difficulty – lack of teacher time to plan and develop a new curriculum – might have been less serious had the school district as a whole been committed to similar change. That would have created less pressure on a single school to develop new curricula, and would have made it politically easier for the school to ask for extra resources to support such development work. Another cost of being an isolated case is that outside organisations such as the university have shown variable support for Chiron's community-based activities: the teachers believe that there is a lack of commitment to the school at the top of such organisations. Thus, there are limits to what a partnership can achieve if it is not part of a system-wide movement for change.

CASE STUDY 16: UNITED KINGDOM

HULL COMPACT – A city-wide job guarantee
"I think it is helping to rebuild the confidence of young people." (Training officer)

The partners

- Hull secondary schools and 6th-form colleges.
- Over 100 Hull employers.
- Hull Compact Company Limited.

The project

Like other compacts in the United States and the United Kingdom, the focus is a "job guarantee" to pupils who meet specific conditions. Students in the fourth and fifth years (ages 14 to 16) are set simple goals covering attendance, punctuality, course completion, work experience, personal and social education, literacy and numeracy, and the keeping of records of achievement. Students who meet the goals may apply for jobs made available in a central "jobs pool" by participating companies, though employers retain final say over whom they hire.

The compact also plays an important role in co-ordinating school-industry links more generally in the city. It matches each school with a representative range of large and small businesses – a form of top-down direction deemed necessary by the recent reorganisation of secondary schooling in the city, which means that every school is new.

The main objectives

"• To generate, through partnership, a better understanding of the world of business and industry.
- Working together to motivate students to develop the attitudes, knowledge and competences necessary to preparation for life and work.
- Rewards will be improved education, training and job opportunities."
(From Compact brochure)

Evolution

The compact was set up in 1988, closely modeled on similar schemes in Boston and London. As the earliest of a series of compacts being set up in British provincial cities, it has in turn attempted to become a model for others. But each compact has also to adapt to local circumstances; in Hull, a city with an economy still fragile after the weakening of its port and manufacturing base,

86

employers proved more hesitant to give firm job pledges than London and Boston firms at times of financial boom. After much negotiation, the company running the compact introduced a system requiring firms to pledge a specified number of jobs, but to retain discretion over specific hiring decisions. Over time, the compact has gradually won the confidence of more and more companies.

Outcomes

The proportion of fifth-year students achieving their compact goals has stabilized at about 42 per cent. Every school-leaver who achieves the goals finds a job with worthwhile training within a few months. The achievement rate may seem disappointing, but has to be set against extremely low levels of educational achievement that have prevailed in the city. The compact organisers believe that many pupils need more time at school to improve their performance, and have procured bursaries of £500 to encourage them. Between 1987 and 1990, the proportion of pupils continuing full-time education after 16 rose from 22 to 34 per cent.

Companies tend to see the compact's most important benefit as improved recruitment efficiency. That benefit helps draw in companies that otherwise might not have links with schools – including for example a city-centre law firm. But once involved, the interest goes much beyond recruitment, and the compact is the focus for a range of work-experience and other link activities, many of them trying to promote a more relevant curriculum.

Comment

The job-guarantee element of the compact has obvious benefits to both sides. Pupils have been given extra motivation – although apparently not enough for over half the students in the city to achieve some simple goals. Employers are given criteria to identify students who are well motivated and might make useful workers even if they do not have good exam results. On the whole, employers appreciate that new indicator.

How does the compact affect partnerships in the city more generally? Most of the links that have developed also exist in cities without compacts. But sometimes their style is subtly different. For example, there are a number of cases where schools consciously offer services to companies in exchange for their involvement in schools. One school, for example, had helped companies by giving *ad hoc* software training through its computer department and by sending a teacher along to carry out a health and safety "audit" with an outsider's eye. The fact that compacts start with a bargain rather than with a one-sided "offer of help" may well foster the idea of *exchange* beyond the job guarantee.

CASE STUDY 17: NETHERLANDS

ROTTERDAM COMPACT – A new route for at-risk pupils

"Education and business are each on an island. We have now built ferries to move between them." (Compact organiser)

The partners

- Lower secondary vocational schools.
- Public and private employers in the metal industry, administration, public services and health care.
- A training institute.
- Agreements with the Chamber of Commerce, Rotterdam City and the national Ministry of Education.

The project

A new method of linking potential drop-outs to the working world at an early stage. Vocational school pupils in their last two years of compulsory education spend three days a week with employers, learning job-specific skills and obtaining a special qualification. Despite similarities to the dual system, participants (aged 15 and 16) keep their status as pupils, and are not apprentices or employees.

The compact office arranges placements by matching pupil profiles provided by the school with participating employers. Students, parents, the training institute and the company draw up a training contract. The training institute ensures that study material is designed to produce the required vocational skills. There is no formal job guarantee, but the expectation is that when the course is completed the student will either be recruited by the company or undergo further education or training. Upper secondary vocational schools have guaranteed places to pupils who meet compact goals.

The compact is part of a wider partnership initiative, the Vrijhaven Project, attempting to strengthen the relationship between training and the labour market in Rotterdam. The project's other main initiative is Rotterdam Regional College, which aims to establish a logistical relationship between all forms of adult education in the Rotterdam region, creating greater cohesion and co-ordination between the courses on offer.

The main objectives

- To tackle the drop-out problem: 30 per cent of vocational students in Rotterdam leave school without qualifications. The compact route aims to provide motivation to stay at school and qualify.
- To bridge the "skills gap": the Rotterdam region has 22 per cent unemployment, yet a shortage of well-trained workers.

Evolution

The city's aldermen and business leaders have been developing a vision of "The New Rotterdam" since the mid-1980s. The Vrijhaven Project was created as a means of co-operation between the public and private sectors in Rotterdam to help the labour market operate more efficiently. In 1989, a delegation from the city visited Boston and wrote a report on its compact. The Rotterdam Compact was launched in September 1991, starting on a small scale with 60 pupils. In its second year it plans to increase this to 100, and eventually may build up to about 300-400, or half the target population of school drop-outs.

Outcomes

A new understanding between vocational schools and employers. This also involves the national government, whose agreement was required to introduce a radically changed curriculum for the participating students.

At the time of writing, it is too early to identify more specific results. But the project is clear on how it will judge its own success: by the number of participants who go into skilled work or further education, having previously been identified as potential drop-outs.

Comment

Rotterdam has created a more focused compact than tends to exist elsewhere. It has not started with a high-profile, universal "job guarantee", but with a new method of working with at-risk pupils, initially few in number. The aim is to earn the confidence of the business community gradually by showing the potential of these students, rather than demanding that firms give guarantees that they might later regret.

One potentially controversial aspect of the scheme is that it concentrates on teaching very specific job skills to 15 and 16 year-olds, when received wisdom says that at this age they should be acquiring broad competences that can be used flexibly. The justification is that these are pupils on the verge of giving up, who more than anything else need motivation. Once the usefulness of learning is demonstrated to them through training in specific jobs, it is hoped that many may return to a broader form of learning.

CASE STUDIES 18 AND 19: UNITED KINGDOM

COMPACTS AND TVEI IN LONDON AND BIRMINGHAM– A tale of two coalitions

These two case studies compare how the interplay between two initiatives can affect the development of partnerships in different areas.

Both London and Birmingham now run locally-based coalitions known as compacts, as well as participating in the national programme known as the Technical and Vocational Education Initiative (TVEI). But whereas London's compact was the spearhead of partnerships, launched before TVEI was introduced into London schools, Birmingham's compact became part of a wider strategy which included the extension of TVEI to all schools. That difference, along with local circumstances, created contrasting partnership styles.

TVEI aims to prepare 14-18 year-olds for transition to working life; to forge close links between education and industry; to raise standards of achievement; to develop interpersonal skills through more interactive teaching and learning styles; to provide in-service training for teachers; to provide work experience for pupils and staff; and to enhance careers guidance by developing individual action plans and records of achievement. So its goals are complementary to those of partnerships and compacts, but its strategy of aiming for long-term change tends to make it more oriented to educational process than to more immediate outputs such as reducing drop-out rates.

CASE STUDY 18: LONDON EDUCATION BUSINESS PARTNERSHIP (LEBP)

"LEBP aims to motivate young people to achieve their full potential in life by enhancing their educational experience." (Compact director)

The partners

- Thirteen Inner London borough education authorities.
- The London Enterprise Agency, representing employers.
- Nine Training and Enterprise Councils (TECs).
- Pupils and parents of Inner London schools and colleges.

The project

A federation of six local compacts. They cover the 14-18 age group and aim to improve achievement of young people in schools and colleges, and to demonstrate the link between this achievement and the ability to secure a worthwhile job.

Employers, schools and colleges each make a commitment to achieve certain goals. Employers agree to provide places for work experience, take teachers on secondment, release staff to visit schools and guarantee jobs for students who meet their compact goals. These goals are: at least 85 per cent attendance and 90 per cent punctuality at school, satisfactory completion of courses in the last two compulsory years, certification in English, maths or numeracy, two weeks' work experience and the completion of the London Record of Achievement.

The main objectives

- To encourage continuing education and/or training for 16 year-olds.
- To motivate students to higher achievements.

Evolution

In 1986 the Partnership was established between the London Enterprise Agency and the Inner London Education Authority (ILEA) to help break down mistrust and hostility between employers and educators. In September 1987 the first compact was launched in East London; by 1991 a total of six had been set up to cover most of the Inner London area – whose education has been in the hands of the boroughs since ILEA's abolition in 1990. TVEI, which has been a major stimulus and source of money for education-industry links across the rest of the country, was only being introduced into London towards the end of this period: it had earlier been blocked by political opposition.

Outcomes

A steep rise in the proportion of 16 year-olds staying on at school in Compact schools:

- On average in Inner London, 45 per cent of 16 year-olds stayed on in 1988/89.
- In the six East London Compact schools, 36.5 per cent stayed on in 1987/88, 55.3 per cent in 1988/89 and 57.3 per cent in 1989/90.
- Of students reaching their "compact goals", 57 per cent stayed on in 1987/88, 76.4 per cent in 1988/89 and 80.3 per cent in 1989/90.

This factor has caused the original goal of guaranteeing a job with training at age 16 to be modified; now there is more emphasis on continuing education and training.

The LEBP is now developing a number of projects to encourage further the active involvement of employers in the work-related curriculum for pupils aged 14 to 18. It is also piloting a 16-19 Careership Compact with more emphasis on further education colleges and the development of core skills (communication, problem-solving, personal skills, numeracy, information technology and modern language competence) across the curriculum for students of *all* abilities.

Comment

See case study 19.

CASE STUDY 19: BIRMINGHAM COMPACT

"Together we are committed to action to improve the opportunities and achievements of our young people." (Compact director)

The partners

- Employers, teachers, students and parents in Birmingham.
- The local authority, the Training and Enterprise Council (TEC), further and higher education institutions, the careers service, TVEI organisers.

The project

A four-year compact to bring about a coalition of all the strategic partners to give young people access to worthwhile jobs and training opportunities within the Birmingham area.

The main objectives

- To improve attainment levels and self-confidence of young people.
- To meet employers' need for a well-qualified and motivated workforce.
- To increase the percentage of pupils who continue their education beyond the minimum school-leaving age.
- To promote equal opportunities.

Evolution

The Birmingham Compact built on an existing Birmingham Education Business Partnership and was launched in September 1989 as part of the national government's Compacts in Inner Cities Initiative. The extension of TVEI to all schools began in Birmingham in the same year, and the two initiatives have taken care to reinforce each other's efforts.

The compact began very small, with only three schools in a single deprived district, but is planned to be spread progressively over the whole city by 1993. Birmingham's TEC, launched in 1990, enthusiastically took up the compact's cause and provided additional money. The local education authority is now financing a project to add a higher education option to the compact.

Outcomes

A six-monthly review assesses progress towards goals by pupils, schools/colleges and employers. The review is used to guide continuous improvement. Quantitative measures are limited, but show encouraging results in terms of pupils' progress in meeting compact goals over the first two terms of the final compulsory year:

From 55 to 77 per cent for coursework;

From 61 to 82 per cent in attendance;

From 88 to 98 per cent in punctuality.

The July 1990 review revealed that 66 per cent of employers were meeting or exceeding their commitments.

Comment (on cases 18 and 19)

There are many similarities between the two cases. Both are in areas of high social and economic deprivation, and ethnic diversity. In both cases, the original initiative for doing something to promote better education-industry co-operation was backed by a large well-established family firm – Whitbread's in London and Cadbury's in Birmingham. Both initiatives were taken up and financed at a later stage by the government.

London, however, suffers from being enormous, with a wide travel-to-work area and diverging employers needs. The abolition of a single education authority in Inner London, to be replaced by 13 small ones, the fact that there are nine TECs (rather than one in Birmingham) and that these and TVEI only appeared well after the establishment of a compact, made London's an uphill battle. It responded with bold initiatives, and by working out strategies as it went along, producing some remarkable partnership deals. The absence of TVEI made the changes that it produced all the more dramatic. As TVEI and TECs enter the picture, this project will undoubtedly become a well-grounded strategic coalition, as long as the "rules of the game" set by government do not change too often.

Birmingham worked towards a strategic coalition, involving all relevant people and programmes, from the start. It has been less bold and more cautious than London, but has had the strong advantage of a more self-contained site, where a single TEC and a single education authority work closely together to plan a network of partnerships which have compact goals and build on TVEI good practice. It has recognised that much link activity already exists between schools and employers, and that it needs to build on this with a clear focus on student achievement matched to the realities of the local employment scene.

CASE STUDY 20: CANADA

"LET'S GRADUATE GEORGINA" – High-school retention in Ontario

"In true community development fashion this is a process-oriented approach to significant intervention, and tangible results will not always be identified immediately." (Project prospectus)

The partners

- York Region Education/Industry Foundation.
- Sutton District High School, in the small town of Georgina, Ontario.
- Twenty social services agencies.
- Ten media representatives.
- Over 60 businesses and the Georgina Board of Trade.
- Parents, clubs, individuals.

The project

An attempt to reduce the town's school drop-out rate by encouraging all sections of the community to participate in creating innovative programmes. Each year over 800 "at risk" 9th-graders (age 14) are identified. Strategies focus in particular on mentoring, individual and group counselling and career assessment.

A committee including students, teachers, parents, employers, social service groups and politicians attempts to assess needs and develop potential student programmes. One such programme, a "satellite night school", tries to communicate the importance of graduation and to bring school out to the community on three satellite locations.

The main objectives

"• To identify and involve all stakeholders in the community in meeting together to find solutions to the drop-out problem.
- To market the model to other communities with high drop-out rates."

Evolution

The programme was established in September 1988, at the initiative of the Education/Industry Foundation. It was a response to the high drop-out rate throughout Ontario, of 30 per cent. In the project's first year, the Foundation raised over C\$ 500 000 from the private sector, much of which was spent on establishing a sophisticated careers centre with modern equipment.

Outcomes

"Initial statistics show that the drop-out rate has fallen", but figures remain vague.

"There has been a dramatic increase of integration and communication between all sectors in the Georgina Community on the central issue of reducing the drop-out rate." For example, social services agencies feel that increased communication with the school has enabled them to serve the needs of high-risk students more effectively. Business people acknowledge the value of closer links with education and the impact this will have on the quality of their future employees.

Comment

The actual drop-out prevention techniques employed by this scheme – better counselling, careers advice, etc. – are nothing new. The novelty is the scheme's stress on the process of "mobilising the stakeholders", that is, ensuring that all people in the town who have an interest in a successful school system apply themselves to the problem. The implicit idea behind this strategy is that a programme such as careers counselling might look good on paper, but will fail unless people such as employers and teachers work enthusiastically behind it.

The scheme is similar to many in North America in concentrating on the process of coalition-building. It also has in common with many other drop-out prevention schemes the idea that students most need encouragement and guidance to show them the advantages of completing school. But is that enough? Such programmes do not ask whether there is something in the content or style of schooling itself that is causing failure and needs to be changed. Schemes that focus on the partnership process are not on the whole disposed to consider whether there is a fundamental need for change in the system.

CASE STUDY 21: CANADA

OTTAWA-CARLETON LEARNING FOUNDATION – A broad educational alliance

"We are trying to set up a regional example of how you can build a coalition."
(Foundation president)

The partners

- Five school boards.
- Two universities.
- Two community colleges.
- Businesses and labour representatives in the region.

The project

A broad coalition attempting to improve the education system in the Ottawa-Carleton region. An umbrella group for a wide variety of schemes, the Foundation attempts to bring together a fragmented education community to work to common goals. Its initiatives are grouped under five broad headings:

- Philanthropic activities – for example helping to meet the needs of schoolchildren below the poverty line.
- "PARTNERS" – helping schools and others to promote science, engineering and technology.
- Transitions to employment – assisting high-school students who are work- or college-bound, for example by finding educational courses for apprentices.
- Adult employment and equity issues – helping train workers to meet current labour market needs.
- Research and development – exploring the potential for new activities.

The main objectives

"• To build a world-class education system in the Ottawa-Carleton region.
- To increase the interaction among people from educational institutions, government, labour and industry to enhance the effectiveness of the education system in the region.
- To drive change from an education system based on knowledge to one based on generic skills and attitude development."

Evolution

The Foundation originated in 1985. It was a reaction to the severe "balkanisation" of education in the region: there had been little or no co-ordination between institutions, including school boards representing French- and English-speakers, Protestants and Catholics, and the independent-minded universities.

The present president of the Foundation believes that there has been a tendency to support partnership projects in too random a manner, and that the coalition needs to have a firmer sense of direction. In 1990 and 1991 there have been various meetings and seminars of the parties involved in an attempt to turn the Foundation into a "strategic coalition" for change, rather than just a co-ordinating body.

Outcomes

As well as encouraging and supporting the initiatives mentioned above, the coalition has provided a framework for tackling specific educational problems in a way that involves all the agencies concerned. A notable example is the attempt to improve careers guidance. The province had required that teachers should spend 10 per cent of their time advising on careers – yet most of them lacked the necessary industrial experience to make this guidance effective. The coalition was able to find ways of increasing such experience. Another problem arose in exchange programmes, in which engineers were supposed to spend time in classrooms: since they did not have teachers' licenses, the rules prevented them from teaching. Co-ordination with the authorities who set the rules helped resolve this difficulty.

Comment

This is a rare attempt to use a regional coalition to co-ordinate a system-wide change in learning strategies. There is always a danger that a broad coalition will become unfocused in its goals. In this case, there seems to be a common will from business and education leaders to push for system change, yet still some uncertainty about how the coalition can ensure that it produces more than just a series of miscellaneous schemes.

PROJECT LINDHOLMEN – Plans for a "society of knowledge" in Gothenburg

"We keep up with the new demands arising from developments in society." (Director of Education, Gothenburg)

The partners

- The City of Gothenburg.
- The Board of Education.
- The County Labour Board.
- The Regional Employment Training Board.
- University of Gothenburg.
- Chalmers Technical University.
- Companies representing trade, industry and technology.

The project

The placing of education, production and research under one roof to encourage stimulating new relationships between all concerned, and to utilise expensive resources more effectively. Interest groups are to work closely with individual companies to implement basic and advanced training in areas of importance to the Gothenburg region.

The main objectives

- To create modern workforce training and renewal in basic education suited to young people, to employees and to accelerating change in society.
- To find new forms of work organisation and improved working environments.
- To enable partners to make joint use of premises and equipment, administration, information, marketing, personnel, development and on-going training.

Evolution

A new part of the city on the north bank of the river Göta Älv, on the site of former shipyards, is to be redeveloped with industries, housing and services. The Lindholmen project has participated in these plans from the start, making education and training one of the corner-stones of the new community. The first centre started in 1986, developing into a unique joint project in training and production. The main partners have been the City of Gothenburg, Volvo, SKF and the National

Swedish Development Foundation. So far they have created a production-technical centre and a computer centre, as well as research resources specialising on working environment issues.

The final Lindholmen Centre is expected to be completed by the mid-1990s. A number of educational centres will be built: for electrical technology, shipping technique, material handling and the restaurant trade. By 1993 around 4 000 people are expected to be studying and working there. The centre will cover about 80 000 square metres, of which about 45 000 will consist of training facilities, about 20 000 devoted to production and the remainder shared equally between research and services.

Outcomes

Project Lindholmen, it is anticipated, will help improve education and training. It will address the needs of initial education, which is perceived to have become out of date as a result of declining resources and insufficient orientation to the needs of companies. It will also address the training of company staff, which is considered to be aimed too much at immediate needs rather than long-term trends in society and work organisation.

Comment

The starting point for this project has been the desire to create a "society of knowledge". The organisers are trying to take advantage of the rebuilding of a significant portion of the city to develop a flexible environment in which research, education and industry can find different ways of creating "a lifetime of learning". The idea is not to build another "dockland development" or another "campus" or "science park". Rather it is to find a new style for the city which will make its people better prepared to meet future challenges.

CASE STUDY 23: CANADA

THE LEARNING ENRICHMENT FOUNDATION – Community development in Toronto

"Public education cannot sit on the sidelines as spectators of... economic evolution."
(Partnership description)

The partners

- City of York Board of Education (in metropolitan Toronto).
- Local industry, community and educational institutions.
- Four levels of government (city, region, province, federal) as grant-givers.

The project

An educational foundation committed to economic and social development in the community. Will spend about $9 million and employ nearly 600 people in 1991 to work on a variety of schemes aimed particularly at poorly-educated immigrant adults and at small entrepreneurs starting up new businesses. Schemes include:

- A centre that tries to help young welfare recipients into jobs.
- A business opportunity centre offering training in various vocational skills, alongside a "business incubator" helping small new businesses to get started.
- An "adopt-an-industry" scheme sending adult educators into enterprises to assess and address their staff development needs; and
- A network of day-care centres.

All these projects involve educational elements that link with York's Adult Day School, which is funded by the school board and teaches high-school standard courses on community-based sites.

The main objectives

- To provide adults with a variety of relevant learning opportunities.
- To link this learning directly with the world of work.
- To link learning with social and community development.

Evolution

Set up in 1979 at the initiative of the school board, the Foundation was a response to rapid change in the City of York, in particular an influx of largely poor, ill-educated immigrants (42 per

100

cent of the population now speak a language other than English in the home) and rising unemployment. The Foundation was community-oriented from the start, promoting multicultural arts enrichment and child-care services as well as youth employment schemes. Its role has broadened since 1984 when the Federal Department of Employment and Immigration invited it to participate in a "local committee of adjustment" to help the city's economy through a difficult transition. While retaining its interest in non-profit activities, the Foundation has also become involved in trying to help public and private enterprises to identify the learning needs of their workers.

Outcomes

The projects listed above may at first sight seem a somewhat random collection of worthy activities. In fact, the Foundation has been remarkably successful in maintaining links between its various interests, and in particular between its interest in community development and workforce preparation. Each of its activities seems to reinforce another. For example, the day-care centres simultaneously teach a vocational skill to trainees, allow parents to study other courses while their children are being looked after, and are themselves helped by other training schemes such as carpentry (which makes their furniture) and catering (which makes their lunch). Similarly, the coexistence of an office skills training course and a small-business incubator on the same site allows fledgeling companies to use secretarial services provided by trainees.

Comment

This is a highly sophisticated coalition which manages to reconcile the various interests of a number of different actors at community, enterprise and individual level. In some cases this involves building on shared goals: the pool of goodwill towards the day-care centres, for example, is an important source of motivation. In other cases, goals can be very individualised and specific. When one of the city's hospitals seconded a teacher under the "adopt-an-industry" scheme, it aimed specifically to find a way of bringing the literacy skills of its auxiliary staff up to standard to enable them to recognise and safely handle dangerous substances.

A unifying theme is the Foundation's commitment to ensure that adult education and training are made directly relevant to workplace requirements. But in this respect, the scheme suffers a potential weakness. The adult day school operates as a high school, awarding ordinary high school credits for its courses. These are the qualifications that are recognised by employers, and for many adults with basic literacy problems the competences provided in high schools may well be relevant. But how accurately can a high school modeled on teenage learning respond to the needs of adult workers beyond instruction in simple reading and writing skills? The reliance on high school accreditation reflects the dominance of initial schooling even in a situation where new attention is being paid to the learning needs of the adult.

CASE STUDY 24: THE NETHERLANDS

THE "RAUWENHOFF PROCESS" – A national policy initiative

"If the government wants to initiate activity at a decentralised level, it has to remove central barriers." (R.F. Rauwenhoff)

The partners

- The Ministries for Education, Economic Affairs and Social Affairs.
- Captains of industry, directors of educational institutions.
- Employers' organisations and trade unions.

The project

An attempt by the Dutch government to improve the interaction between education and the labour market. The focus has been a committee bringing together the various interests involved, chaired by R.F. Rauwenhoff, then President of Philips Netherlands. The committee proposed greater autonomy for schools, to allow them to forge closer links with the labour market, and more communication between government, business and education. The focus of the proposals was vocational schools.

The main objectives

- To improve links between educational supply and labour market demand.
- To combat high drop-out rates.
- To reduce rules hindering partnerships.
- To counter the bias which favours general over vocational education.

Evolution

The committee was launched by an incoming coalition government in late 1989, and told to present "non-orthodox" recommendations within six months. It reported in May 1990 and the government responded, positively, in October. But this fast-moving process then apparently stalled, as a result of political sensitivity over the accusation that the government's motive was to save public money by getting business to pay for education.

Outcomes

In the summer of 1991, the government was preparing legislation to implement some of the principles set out in the Rauwenhoff committee's report. This is intended, amongst other things, to improve vocational qualifications and to give upper secondary vocational schools fixed budgets based on their enrolment levels, giving them more financial autonomy. Later, it is planned to give similar autonomy to adult vocational colleges, merging these institutions together to make them behave more like American community colleges.

There had also been some action relevant to the Rauwenhoff recommendations before the committee reported. In particular, legislation in 1986 gave schools greater freedom to take actions relevant to their assessment of local labour market needs. There has been a progressive relaxation of rules, strongly influenced but not originated by the Rauwenhoff report.

However, the main results of the Rauwenhoff initiative are less tangible. They include:

- A heightened consciousness among both industrialists and educators of the need for local partnership initiative.
- A relaxing in practice of rules restricting schools from forming autonomous local partnerships.
- The involvement for the first time of the Ministries of Economic and Social Affairs in educational matters. This is not presented as a bid to take over the administration of any sector of education, but rather as an attempt to stimulate change, and improve the poor communications between the private sector and the education authorities.

Comment

The Dutch case confirms that a national government is not in a position to legislate partnerships, but can act as an enabler and stimulater of local initiatives. The most important first step is to identify the greatest barriers to partnership activity: in the Netherlands, over-centralisation of the school system was seen to be the key problem. The raising of such barriers may in itself stimulate partnerships, but there is a danger in a country without a tradition of business-school co-operation that the idea will be slow to take root. In that case, the government might need to become more pro-active, for example by getting involved in schemes that reward certain types of project. (See case study 3 for a British example.) The Netherlands also provides an example of how partnerships within government can be just as important as partnerships between the public and private sectors. Economics and Employment ministries have often been kept well away from the education world. Education ministries fear for their sphere of control, but the Dutch Ministry of Economic Affairs believes it can play a complementary role – finding ways of linking education more closely to business, while leaving the administration of schools to education officials.

Annex 1

ADDRESSES FOR FURTHER INFORMATION

Case 1: Mr. Anthony McLaren
Schools Liaison Manager
Digital Equipment Scotland Ltd.
Mosshill Industrial Estate
Ayr KA6 6BE, GREAT BRITAIN

Cases 2, 8 & 20: Mr. Michael Bloom
The Conference Board of Canada
255 Smyth Road
Ottawa, Ontario KIH 8M7, CANADA

Case 3: Mr. Sidney Slater
SCIP-MESP
Centre for Education and Industry
University of Warwick
Westwood, Coventry, CV4 7AL, GREAT BRITAIN

Case 4: Mr. Alain Bordes
Chambre de Commerce et d'Industrie du Lot
107 Quai Cavaignac, BP 79
46002 Cahors Cedex, FRANCE

Case 5: Mr. Len Wood
Tioxide United Kingdom Ltd.
Moody Lane
Grimsby, DN31 2SW, GREAT BRITAIN

Case 6: Mr. Jeff Baughman
Principal, Chesterfield Technical Center
10101 Court House Road
Chesterfield, Virginia 23832, UNITED STATES

Case 7: Mr. Paul Feilleux
Chargé de Mission
Régie Nationale des Usines Renault
Direction du Personnel et des Affaires Sociales
92109 Boulogne Billancourt Cedex, FRANCE

Case 8:   see case 2

Case 9:   Ms. Vincenzina Guzzi
ITSOS Marie Curie
Via Masaccio
20063 Cernusco sul Naviglio, ITALY

Case 10:   Mr. Günther Klatz
Bundesgymnasium Reutte
Gymnasiumstrasse 10
A-6600 Reutte, Tyrol, AUSTRIA

Case 11:   Mr. Norbert Gudlat
Der Kultusminister NRW
Postfach 1103
4000 Dusseldorf 1, GERMANY

Case 12:   Mr. Jacques Guillaud
Dispositif Ariane
Rectorat, Place Bir-Hakem
38000 Grenoble, FRANCE

Case 13:   Ms. Lesley Bradshaw
North Yorkshire Schools and Industry Association
Park Grove School, Dudley Street
York YO3 7LG, GREAT BRITAIN

Case 14:   The Co-ordinator
Santa Fe Schools Improvement Program
610 Alta Vista Street
Santa Fe, New Mexico 87501, UNITED STATES

Case 15:   Ms. Kathleen Burke
Chiron Middle School
25 North 16th St.
Minneapolis, MN 55403-1229, UNITED STATES

Case 16:   Mr. Barry Salt
Hull Compact
Reckitt House
Stoneferry
Hull HU8 8DD, GREAT BRITAIN

Case 17:   Mr. Ton Peters
P O Box 70016
3000 KV Rotterdam, NETHERLANDS

Cases 18 & 19:   Ms. Anne Jones
23 Southerton Road
London W6 OPJ, GREAT BRITAIN

Case 20:   see case 2

Case 21:   Mr. Mac Prescott
Ottawa-Carleton Learning Foundation
340 March Road, Suite 401
Kanata, Ontario K2K 2E4, CANADA

Case 22:   Mr. Evert Lindholm
Kunskapcentrum Lindholmen
Utbildningsnämnden
Box 5428
S-402 29 Göteborg, SWEDEN

Case 23:   Mr. Dale Shuttleworth
Superintendent of Community Services
City of York Board of Education
2 Trethewey Drive
Toronto, Ontario M6M 4A8, CANADA

Case 24:   Dr. A. Ijzerman
Directie Beroepsonderwijs en Volwasseneneducatie
Ministerie van Onderwijs en Wetenschappen
Europaweg 4
Postbus 25000
2700 LZ Zoetermeer, NETHERLANDS

CERI EXPERT GROUP ON EDUCATION-BUSINESS PARTNERSHIPS, 1990-1991

Mr. Colin Ball, Consultant, United Kingdom

Mr. Jeff Baughman, Principal, Chesterfield Technical Center, Virginia, United States

Mr. Andréas Botsch, Assistant Secretary-General, TUAC

Ms. Florence Campbell, Vice President, Conference Board of Canada

Mr. Keith Davies, Manager, External European Education Programmes, IBM-Europe

Mr. Denis Doyle, Hudson Institute, United States

Mr. Paul Feilleux, Chargé de Mission, Renault, France

Ms. Monica Frish, Personnel Planning and Strategy Development, IBM-Europe

Mr. Björn Grunewald, Chairman, BIAC Education Committee

Mr. Kazuhiro Hayashi, First Secretary, Permanent Delegation of Japan to the OECD

Ms. Anne Jones, Director of Education, Department of Employment, United Kingdom

Ms. Kerstin Keen, Volvo Competence Development Corporation, Sweden

Mr. Kerry Keogh, Counsellor, Permanent Delegation of Australia to the OECD

Mr. Chris Marsden, Head of Educational Affairs, BP, United Kingdom

Mr. Jan-Peter Paul, Director, Helsinki Institute, Finland

Mr. Livio Pescia, Istituto per la Ricostruzione Industriale, Italy

Mr. Karel van Rosmalan, Ministry of Economic Affairs, Netherlands

Mr. Dale Shuttleworth, Superintendent of Community Services, City of York Board of Education, Toronto, Canada

Mr. Mike Smith, Human Resources Manager, Tioxide Group PLC, United Kingdom

Mr. René Tijou, Directeur de la Formation et du Développement Social, Renault, France

Mr. David Turner, Human Resources Manager (Development), Tioxide Group PLC, United Kingdom

Mr. Marc van der Varst, Ministry of Education, Netherlands

Mr. Erik Wallin, Dean of Social Sciences, University of Upsala, Sweden

Mr. Fred Wentzel, Vice President and Corporate Secretary, National Alliance of Business, United States.

MAIN SALES OUTLETS OF OECD PUBLICATIONS – PRINCIPAUX POINTS DE VENTE DES PUBLICATIONS DE L'OCDE

Argentina – Argentine
Carlos Hirsch S.R.L.
Galería Güemes, Florida 165, 4° Piso
1333 Buenos Aires   Tel. (1) 331.1787 y 331.2391
                        Telefax: (1) 331.1787

Australia – Australie
D.A. Book (Aust.) Pty. Ltd.
648 Whitehorse Road, P.O.B 163
Mitcham, Victoria 3132   Tel. (03) 873.4411
                            Telefax: (03) 873.5679

Austria – Autriche
OECD Publications and Information Centre
Schedestrasse 7
D-W 5300 Bonn 1 (Germany)   Tel. (49.228) 21.60.45
                                Telefax: (49.228) 26.11.04

Gerold & Co.
Graben 31
Wien I   Tel. (0222) 533.50.14

Belgium – Belgique
Jean De Lannoy
Avenue du Roi 202
B-1060 Bruxelles   Tel. (02) 538.51.69/538.08.41
                       Telefax: (02) 538.08.41

Canada
Renouf Publishing Company Ltd.
1294 Algoma Road
Ottawa, ON K1B 3W8   Tel. (613) 741.4333
                         Telefax: (613) 741.5439
Stores:
61 Sparks Street
Ottawa, ON K1P 5R1   Tel. (613) 238.8985
211 Yonge Street
Toronto, ON M5B 1M4   Tel. (416) 363.3171

Federal Publications
165 University Avenue
Toronto, ON M5H 3B8   Tel. (416) 581.1552
                          Telefax: (416)581.1743

Les Éditions La Liberté Inc.
3020 Chemin Sainte-Foy
Sainte-Foy, PQ G1X 3V6   Tel. (418) 658.3763
                             Telefax: (418) 658.3763

China – Chine
China National Publications Import
  Export Corporation (CNPIEC)
P.O. Box 88
Beijing   Tel. 44.0731
              Telefax: 401.5661

Denmark – Danemark
Munksgaard Export and Subscription Service
35, Nørre Søgade, P.O. Box 2148
DK-1016 København K   Tel. (33) 12.85.70
                          Telefax: (33) 12.93.87

Finland – Finlande
Akateeminen Kirjakauppa
Keskuskatu 1, P.O. Box 128
00100 Helsinki   Tel. (358 0) 12141
                     Telefax: (358 0) 121.4441

France
OECD/OCDE
Mail Orders/Commandes par correspondance:
2, rue André-Pascal
75775 Paris Cédex 16   Tel. (33-1) 45.24.82.00
                           Telefax: (33-1) 45.24.85.00
                           or (33-1) 45.24.81.76
                           Telex: 620 160 OCDE

Bookshop/Librairie:
33, rue Octave-Feuillet
75016 Paris   Tel. (33-1) 45.24.81.67
                  (33-1) 45.24.81.81

Librairie de l'Université
12a, rue Nazareth
13100 Aix-en-Provence   Tel. 42.26.18.08
                            Telefax: 42.26.63.26

Germany – Allemagne
OECD Publications and Information Centre
Schedestrasse 7
D-W 5300 Bonn 1   Tel. (0228) 21.60.45
                      Telefax: (0228) 26.11.04

Greece – Grèce
Librairie Kauffmann
Mavrokordatou 9
106 78 Athens   Tel. 322.21.60
                    Telefax: 363.39.67

Hong Kong
Swindon Book Co. Ltd.
13 - 15 Lock Road
Kowloon, Hong Kong   Tel. 366.80.31
                         Telefax: 739.49.75

Iceland – Islande
Mál Mog Menning
Laugavegi 18, Pósthólf 392
121 Reykjavik   Tel. 162.35.23

India – Inde
Oxford Book and Stationery Co.
Scindia House
New Delhi 110001   Tel.(11) 331.5896/5308
                       Telefax: (11) 332.5993

17 Park Street
Calcutta 700016   Tel. 240832

Indonesia – Indonésie
Pdii-Lipi
P.O. Box 269/JKSMG/88
Jakarta 12790   Tel. 583467
                    Telex: 62 875

Ireland – Irlande
TDC Publishers – Library Suppliers
12 North Frederick Street
Dublin 1   Tel. 74.48.35/74.96.77
               Telefax: 74.84.16

Israel
Electronic Publications only
Publications électroniques seulement
Sophist Systems Ltd.
71 Allenby Street
Tel-Aviv 65134   Tel. 3-29.00.21
                     Telefax: 3-29.92.39

Italy – Italie
Libreria Commissionaria Sansoni
Via Duca di Calabria 1/1
50125 Firenze   Tel. (055) 64.54.15
                    Telefax: (055) 64.12.57
Via Bartolini 29
20155 Milano   Tel. (02) 36.50.83
Editrice e Libreria Herder
Piazza Montecitorio 120
00186 Roma   Tel. 679.46.28
                 Telex: NATEL I 621427

Libreria Hoepli
Via Hoepli 5
20121 Milano   Tel. (02) 86.54.46
                   Telefax: (02) 805.28.86

Libreria Scientifica
Dott. Lucio de Biasio 'Aeiou'
Via Meravigli 16
20123 Milano   Tel. (02) 805.68.98
                   Telefax: (02) 80.01.75

Japan – Japon
OECD Publications and Information Centre
Landic Akasaka Building
2-3-4 Akasaka, Minato-ku
Tokyo 107   Tel. (81.3) 3586.2016
                Telefax: (81.3) 3584.7929

Korea – Corée
Kyobo Book Centre Co. Ltd.
P.O. Box 1658, Kwang Hwa Moon
Seoul   Tel. 730.78.91
            Telefax: 735.00.30

Malaysia – Malaisie
Co-operative Bookshop Ltd.
University of Malaya
P.O. Box 1127, Jalan Pantai Baru
59700 Kuala Lumpur
Malaysia   Tel. 756.5000/756.5425
               Telefax: 757.3661

Netherlands – Pays-Bas
SDU Uitgeverij
Christoffel Plantijnstraat 2
Postbus 20014
2500 EA's-Gravenhage   Tel. (070 3) 78.99.11
Voor bestellingen: Tel. (070 3) 78.98.80
                           Telefax: (070 3) 47.63.51

New Zealand – Nouvelle-Zélande
GP Publications Ltd.
Customer Services
33 The Esplanade - P.O. Box 38-900
Petone, Wellington   Tel. (04) 5685.555
                         Telefax: (04) 5685.333

Norway – Norvège
Narvesen Info Center - NIC
Bertrand Narvesens vei 2
P.O. Box 6125 Etterstad
0602 Oslo 6   Tel. (02) 57.33.00
                  Telefax: (02) 68.19.01

Pakistan
Mirza Book Agency
65 Shahrah Quaid-E-Azam
Lahore 3   Tel. 66.839
               Telex: 44886 UBL PK. Attn: MIRZA BK

Portugal
Livraria Portugal
Rua do Carmo 70-74
Apart. 2681
1117 Lisboa Codex   Tel.: (01) 347.49.82/3/4/5
                        Telefax: (01) 347.02.64

Singapore – Singapour
Information Publications Pte. Ltd.
Pei-Fu Industrial Building
24 New Industrial Road No. 02-06
Singapore 1953   Tel. 283.1786/283.1798
                     Telefax: 284.8875

Spain – Espagne
Mundi-Prensa Libros S.A.
Castelló 37, Apartado 1223
Madrid 28001   Tel. (91) 431.33.99
                   Telefax: (91) 575.39.98

Libreria Internacional AEDOS
Consejo de Ciento 391
08009 - Barcelona   Tel. (93) 488.34.92
                        Telefax: (93) 487.76.59

Llibreria de la Generalitat
Palau Moja
Rambla dels Estudis, 118
08002 - Barcelona   Tel. (93) 318.80.12 (Subscripcions)
                        (93) 302.67.23 (Publicacions)
                        Telefax: (93) 412.18.54

Sri Lanka
Centre for Policy Research
c/o Colombo Agencies Ltd.
No. 300-304, Galle Road
Colombo 3   Tel. (1) 574240, 573551-2
                Telefax: (1) 575394, 510711

Sweden – Suède
Fritzes Fackboksföretaget
Box 16356
Regeringsgatan 12
103 27 Stockholm   Tel. (08) 23.89.00
                       Telefax: (08) 20.50.21

Subscription Agency/Abonnements:
Wennergren-Williams AB
Nordenflychtsvägen 74
Box 30004
104 25 Stockholm   Tel. (08) 13.67.00
                       Telefax: (08) 618.62.32

Switzerland – Suisse
OECD Publications and Information Centre
Schedestrasse 7
D-W 5300 Bonn 1 (Germany)   Tel. (49.228) 21.60.45
                                Telefax: (49.228) 26.11.04

Suisse romande
Maditec S.A.
Chemin des Palettes 4
1020 Renens/Lausanne   Tel. (021) 635.08.65
                           Telefax: (021) 635.07.80

Librairie Payot
6 rue Grenus
1211 Genève 11   Tel. (022) 731.89.50
                     Telex: 28356

Subscription Agency – Service des Abonnements
Naville S.A.
7, rue Lévrier
1201 Genève   Tél.: (022) 732.24.00
                  Telefax: (022) 738.87.13

Taiwan – Formose
Good Faith Worldwide Int'l. Co. Ltd.
9th Floor, No. 118, Sec. 2
Chung Hsiao E. Road
Taipei   Tel. (02) 391.7396/391.7397
             Telefax: (02) 394.9176

Thailand – Thaïlande
Suksit Siam Co. Ltd.
113, 115 Fuang Nakhon Rd.
Opp. Wat Rajbopith
Bangkok 10200   Tel. (662) 251.1630
                    Telefax: (662) 236.7783

Turkey – Turquie
Kültur Yayinlari Is-Türk Ltd. Sti.
Atatürk Bulvari No. 191/Kat. 21
Kavaklidere/Ankara   Tel. 25.07.60
Dolmabahce Cad. No. 29
Besiktas/Istanbul   Tel. 160.71.88
                        Telex: 43482B

United Kingdom – Royaume-Uni
HMSO
Gen. enquiries   Tel. (071) 873 0011
Postal orders only:
P.O. Box 276, London SW8 5DT
Personal Callers HMSO Bookshop
49 High Holborn, London WC1V 6HB
                        Telefax: 071 873 2000
Branches at: Belfast, Birmingham, Bristol, Edinburgh,
                        Manchester

United States – États-Unis
OECD Publications and Information Centre
2001 L Street N.W., Suite 700
Washington, D.C. 20036-4910   Tel. (202) 785.6323
                                  Telefax: (202) 785.0350

Venezuela
Libreria del Este
Avda F. Miranda 52, Aptdo. 60337
Edificio Galipán
Caracas 106   Tel. 951.1705/951.2307/951.1297
                  Telegram: Libreste Caracas

Yugoslavia – Yougoslavie
Jugoslovenska Knjiga
Knez Mihajlova 2, P.O. Box 36
Beograd   Tel. (011) 621.992
              Telefax: (011) 625.970

Orders and inquiries from countries where Distributors have
not yet been appointed should be sent to: OECD Publications Service, 2 rue André-Pascal, 75775 Paris Cédex 16,
France.

Les commandes provenant de pays où l'OCDE n'a pas
encore désigné de distributeur devraient être adressées à :
OCDE, Service des Publications, 2, rue André-Pascal, 75775
Paris Cédex 16, France.

370.19316 Hir
Hirsch, Donald.
Schools and business

OECD PUBLICATIONS, 2 rue André-Pascal, 75775 PARIS CEDEX 16
PRINTED IN FRANCE
(96 92 01 1) ISBN 92-64-13632-0 - No. 45931 1992

X